MW01611920

renew your mind

40 DAYS TO QUIET THE LIES INSIDE YOUR HEAD

dear *friend,*

We pray these devotions bring you hope and encouragement as you process your thoughts through the lens of God's love and His good plans for you.

This devotional is designed to help you work through the sometimes hard and worrisome thoughts we all have. It's normal for all of us to feel fear, worry and anxiety at times. We may also go through seasons of grief that last longer than we expect. And we have thoughts that surprise us in their intensity.

We also want to acknowledge that some thoughts you have might be more concerning, and you wonder whether you have the tools to process them on your own or whether you might need help.

In cases like that, it's good to talk to a doctor, professional counselor or therapist. A professional can help if your thoughts feel all-consuming, cause you overwhelming or prolonged distress, or make it hard to fulfill your daily obligations. And if you feel like acting on your thoughts could harm you or others, please seek help right away.

Life can be incredibly hard, and there are times you might feel utterly without hope. We want you to know: There is hope and help for your situation. God loves you so deeply and offers grace and strength in times of need.

We've put some professional resources at the back of this book if you would like a trusted recommendation for help.

God bless you,

Your friends at Proverbs 31 Ministries

table *of* contents

When Innocent Thoughts Become Demanding Dictators
SHIRLEE ABBOTT

"Let the words of my mouth and the meditation of my heart be acceptable in your sight, O LORD, my rock and my redeemer." Psalm 19:14 (ESV)

I start each day with the best intentions, trying to think good thoughts. But reality gets in my way.

Alone in my car, I practice self-righteous speeches to someone who hurt me or a co-worker who hijacked my good idea. Silently on my bed, I fantasize about a Pinterest-perfect house or a rom-com relationship.

Does this sound familiar? Do thoughts that initially seem justified or innocent start you on a path to bitterness, envy or despair? The psalmist who wrote Psalm 19 saw the risk and prayed these words to God:

"Keep back your servant also from presumptuous sins; let them not have dominion over me!" (Psalm 19:13a, ESV).

It seems clear that *"presumptuous sins,"* built on willful, rebellious thoughts, can *"have dominion"* over us. They can grab control ... but God can free us from these unwelcome intruders.

Picture your mind as a harbor: Thoughts sail in and out. You invite some to drop anchor and stay at your home. At first, a thought may seem harmless. You entertain it. You even serve it fresh-from-the-oven chocolate chip cookies. You share some innocent conversation. You laugh together. But gradually, this thought morphs from friendly guest to demanding dictator. It wants bigger chunks of your time. It seeps beyond the boundaries of your self-control. It distorts your attitudes and actions.

For me, it works like this:
Co-workers reject my idea and get behind a colleague's suggestion. I think: *My idea is better. I hope hers fails.* ***I'll make sure it doesn't work.***

I watch home improvement shows. I think: *My kitchen is boring. I wish I had a fancy new one like those on TV.* ***Our home is so bad — why bother?***

Something I said doesn't feel right. I think: *That didn't come out the way I intended. It was a stupid thing to say.* **I can't do anything right.**

Do you see how a sneaky thought takes over? I no longer control the thought. It tries to control me, leading me to sin.

The longer I harbor a negative or sinful thought, the more control it tries to take, and the harder it is to make it leave.

Hundreds of thoughts sail through our minds. How do we know which ones will prove to be troublemakers? The psalmist continued his prayer:

"Let the words of my mouth and the meditation of my heart be acceptable in your sight, O Lord, my rock and my redeemer" (Psalm 19:14).

"The meditation of my heart" consists of the thoughts that sail in and out of my mind. *"Acceptable"* means pleasing, desirable to God.

Try this: Picture yourself sitting at the table with Jesus, sharing coffee, cookies, and one of these new thoughts below. Does He nod His approval? Or does He say something different?

"So whatever you wish that others would do to you, do also to them ... " (Matthew 7:12a, ESV).

"... Be content with what you have ... " (Hebrews 13:5, ESV).

"For we are his workmanship, created in Christ Jesus for good works ... " (Ephesians 2:10, ESV).

Good news! Ungodly thoughts don't like to share space with Christ. Invite Him to the conversation. Those negative thoughts might pull up their anchor and sail off on their own. And even if they don't, you have Jesus on your side.

Lord God, let's talk about my thoughts. Give me eyes to see Your nod of approval when my thoughts are good. Give me ears to hear Your words of correction when they're not. Teach me to harbor thoughts that are pleasing in Your sight. Grant me wisdom to recognize negative thoughts and send them on their way before they drop anchor. Banish ungodly thoughts from the harbor of my mind. In Jesus' Name, Amen.

Whodunit? Exposing the Enemy of Our Souls

SARAH MCCLELLAND

"The thief comes only to steal and kill and destroy. I came that they may have life and have it abundantly." John 10:10 (ESV)

I love mysteries. Something about the thrilling chase, perplexing clues and cunning characters keeps me on the edge of my seat. I've got to know "whodunit"!

While I always enjoy solving fictional crimes, I often find it far more challenging to unravel the false narratives and twisted tales in my own mind. Unlike a book I can put down at any time, my fears, insecurities and shame seem to follow me everywhere like a bandit bent on harm.

Some of the lies in my head are old. So old they've gathered dust like a book untouched for ages. No doubt, I've read that book so many times I've memorized it and laid it to rest with my everyday décor. It reminds me daily of how worthless and unlovable I really am ... or so I tell myself again and again and again.

When our negative thought patterns become deeply rooted, like bad habits, they seem normal. So we live with them. We don't always stop to think about what's behind our thoughts or whether they're true. If we've always believed them, they must be true, right?

What if the result of believing lies is more serious than we think? Sure, we've learned to live with them. But what if they keep us from experiencing the fullness of the lives we were meant to live?

Consider John 10:10, where Jesus said, *"The thief comes only to steal and kill and destroy. I came that they may have life and have it abundantly."*

While we know Jesus is the One who died so we could have abundant life, we must wonder: Who is the thief in this passage? Who is the enemy of our souls, and what is he trying to steal?

Scripture tells us Satan is the thief. He's the father of all lies (John 8:44), the man with the mask, hiding behind every accusation (Revelation 12:10), every ounce of shame and condemnation thrown at you, every sudden reminder that people said you would never amount to anything.

Like a bandit bent on stealing our joy, peace and freedom (i.e., abundant life), the devil constantly searches for ways to bring us down. He doesn't want us to fully embrace the truth of who we are in Christ.

Why? Because the truth is dangerous for him. It's what reveals his plot. It's what allows us to have peace and joy in any circumstance. It also equips us to walk fully in the callings God has given us — something Satan trembles to think about.

God's Truth is our spiritual weapon. Rather than fighting the battle outwardly and endlessly trying harder to "be better," we fight lies inwardly. By renewing our minds with the Word of God (Romans 12:2), we remind ourselves of who God says we already are, not who our enemy accuses us of being.

Abundant life in Christ is available, no matter what the devil has told you or how many times you've heard it. And abundance starts with renewing our minds with God's Word.

Lord, I confess I've let the enemy tell me who I am for a long time. I've gotten used to believing the accusations and living with fear, shame and insecurity. Please help me to uncover each lie that is keeping me from the abundant life You offer. Help me renew my mind in each area and overcome the enemy of my soul. I trust in You and know You will guide me in Your Truth. In Jesus' Name, Amen.

Your Focus Determines Your Direction
MEGAN WILCZEK

"... For we have no power to face this vast army that is attacking us. We do not know what to do, but our eyes are on you." 2 Chronicles 20:12 (NIV)

Where I live in rural Wisconsin, it's fairly normal to see a deer hanging out on the road. Obviously, no one wants to hit a deer with their car. Unfortunately, there's this subconscious rule of life that you'll go in the direction you look.

This is called "target fixation." So if you're looking at the deer, you're more likely to drive toward it, even when you want to avoid it.

Have you noticed a similar pattern with our minds? What we focus on is what we go toward, even if we don't want to. It's kind of like when I once tried to avoid eating sweets. Before I knew it, there I was in the pantry, eating cookies. I was so focused on not eating the cookies that the cookies were constantly on my mind!

In 2 Chronicles 20, King Jehoshaphat, the king of Judah, had a different focus: one that sent him in the right direction.

He was facing a great war and stood in front of an assembly of his people, praying, *"Our God, will you not judge them? For we have no power to face this vast army that is attacking us. We do not know what to do, but our eyes are on you"* (2 Chronicles 20:12).

The king and his people chose to focus on *God* rather than *the war* they faced. They decided to give thanks to God before the battle had even started. As they marched to war, they had men marching ahead of them praising God. By the time the king and his men arrived at the battle, the other armies, who were targeting Judah, had turned against and killed each other. God had already won the battle by the time Jehoshaphat arrived (2 Chronicles 20:20-26).

So the next time your thoughts seem to be spinning out of control, instead of trying to focus on how to make the toxic thoughts stop, focus on God. Keep your eyes on Him until you run straight into Him. Praise Him before the battle is even won. Thank Him for helping you overcome this. Make target fixation work to your benefit.

We can't empty our minds of fear and expect it to stay away if we don't fill that space with something else. Thankfully, we can fill our minds with Scripture, prayer, praise, God's promises and God's holiness.

Those toxic thoughts will try to weasel their way back in, but just tell yourself, *Girl, we don't have time for that.* Then turn your attention back to God. Don't condemn yourself for having negative thoughts again — but as far as you're able, don't allow them to take up any more space in your mind.

Dear God, thank You for Your goodness. Please help me to focus on You and the good things You have blessed me with. Remind me to praise You even before the battle has been won. By myself, I am powerless in this battle, but all my power in this life comes from You. Keep me close to You, and don't allow me to wander or slip away. Thank You for everything You have done for me. In Jesus' Name, Amen.

Guarding the Source of Everything

MARLENE JAMES

"Above all else, guard your heart, for everything you do flows from it."
Proverbs 4:23 (NIV)

Sometimes I get in a mood. A funk. I argue with everything I hear. I disagree with everything I read. I criticize everything I see.

My feelings are justified in my mind. Because of something. Because of everything.

Bad day. Work. Kids.
What she said. The way it was said. Or wasn't.
Tired. Busy. Can't sleep.
News. Social media. Chatter.
Not fair. Sorry. Not sorry.
Attitudes. Meltdowns.
Wrong. Fault. Guilt.
All. Things.

Or maybe it's because I'm not guarding my heart.

God gave us a way to redirect our moods and attitudes, and it starts in the heart: *"Above all else, guard your heart, for everything you do flows from it"* (Proverbs 4:23).

When my youngest was a little tot, I would ask her what was in her heart. She would always joyfully reply, "CHICKEN!" I am not sure what spills from a heart full of chicken. However, I do know that when I don't guard my heart, the enemy's lies fill and flow from it.

If I am not prepared to guard my heart, I can feel agitation swell into the very places of my life that I love most, that I need, that sustain me. When I start judging, grumbling and whining, I also start to struggle to be productive, to speak kind words, to provide encouragement, and to live and love like Jesus.

When life is a lot, it's easy to ignore what is happening to our hearts. One negative thought becomes a negative word … which becomes a negative conversation … which becomes a negative attitude … which becomes negative actions and negative words. And there it is: a funk.

In our neglect, the enemy sees an opening. He takes hold, and before we know it, our hearts become more and more hardened. If we are not in a position to receive God's truths, we will fall for the enemy's lies. They are everywhere, and they are loud.

Being intentional in guarding our hearts has everything to do with what we allow to fill our hearts. Chicken probably won't do much for our hearts, but these things will:

> ❧ **God's Word and His promises.** Stay close to God through prayer, reading your Bible, looking for His goodness and listening to His Truth. He is, was and will be with you.

> ❧ **Loved ones.** Surround yourself with people who truly love and support you. Not everyone in your circle is part of your village; know the difference, and keep your village close.

> ❧ **Grace.** Give it freely to others as well as yourself.

Even if the enemy is trying to fill our hearts with the fear, hatred, demands and sadness that the world is so full of, we can rest assured in the love of God and His blessings that will not only fill our hearts but overflow into every part of our lives.

Father God, we come to You with hearts heavy with ugly junk from the day. When our hearts are not in a position to receive Your goodness, we get so tangled in webs of the enemy's lies. We pray for forgiveness for allowing that deceit to filter into our hearts and spill into decisions that do not glorify You. Help us not only to guard our hearts but to fill our hearts with Your hope, love and peace. In Jesus' Name, Amen.

God Replaces Our Weakness With His Strength

KELLY BASHAM

"Because the Sovereign Lord helps me, I will not be disgraced. Therefore have I set my face like flint, and I know I will not be put to shame." Isaiah 50:7 (NIV)

It happened again. While I was lying in my bed, comfy and starting to fall asleep, the thought that I'd made an error on something popped into my head and jarred me awake.

My heart raced, my palms began sweating, and my chest suddenly felt like a heavy stone was resting upon it. *What is wrong with me?* I felt helpless to control the panicky sensations that engulfed me or the troublesome thoughts that flooded my mind.

Later, my doctor said I was experiencing anxiety attacks, likely triggered by stress. Discovering I'd been struggling with anxiety for years brought new worries.

Why can't I handle things like everyone else?
What will everyone think if they find out about my anxiety?
What does God think about my weakness?

I felt inadequate and like a failure. Most of all, I felt ashamed and believed myself too broken and weak to serve God in any capacity.

In 2 Corinthians, we read that Paul also experienced weakness. The Scriptures don't give many details, but Bible scholars believe there could have been a mental or physical ailment or a besetting sin he struggled with.

Despite Paul's pleas for God to remove his weakness, God didn't take it away (2 Corinthians 12:7-9). Instead, God told Paul, *"My grace is sufficient for you, for my power is made perfect in weakness"* (2 Corinthians 12:9a, NIV). Content with God's answer, Paul expressed he would delight in his weaknesses for the sake of Christ (2 Corinthians 12:10).

But delighting in our weaknesses is no easy feat. And we have an enemy, the devil, who is waiting for an opportunity to strike (1 Peter 5:8). He doesn't want us to delight in our weaknesses; he'd rather we fear them.

Fear stimulates doubt, and the enemy knows it. He whispers lies to emphasize our frailties, shaming us into believing God wouldn't choose us to help further His Kingdom.

But we belong to a God who gives grace, not shame. Isaiah 50:7 says, *"Because the Sovereign LORD helps me ... I will not be put to shame."*

We all have areas of weakness, and like Paul, we may always have them. The enemy would have us believe the lie that we are exempt from being valuable to God because of our flaws, but the opposite is true: Our dependence on God accentuates His grace, power and glory.

When we start to think we can't be of use to God for any reason, let's *"set [our] face like flint,"* as Isaiah 50:7 says, and determine to walk unashamedly in the grace God gives, humbly relying on Him and trusting He will enable us to do the good work He created us to do, as He works through our weaknesses (Ephesians 2:10).

Lord, I thank You that I can come to You for help. Your Word tells me You will not let me be put to shame. When the enemy whispers his lies and I start to fear that You can't use me, help me remember that You can work through my weaknesses and are glorified through my dependence on You. Thank You, Lord, for Your grace and mercy. I'm so grateful I can walk unashamedly in the grace You give. In Jesus' Name, Amen.

Relinquishing Your Role as "The Fixer"

BONNIE DOROUGH

"The LORD is my strength and my shield; My heart trusted in Him, and I am helped; Therefore my heart greatly rejoices, And with my song I will praise Him." Psalm 28:7 (NKJV)

As my teen daughter walked through the mudroom door after school, her solemn face told the tale of a hard day: a test that didn't go well and friends who didn't quite meet her expectations of being friendly.

What's a girl to do? And what's a mom to do?

I can fix this, I thought. *I'll cheer her up, help her push past this emotional thunderstorm, and everyone will be happy. It's all up to me. Because if I don't do it … who will?*

Sometimes, especially as women, we experience self-made pressure to be the glue of our families. We attempt to restore peace as we try to fix everyone's emotional issues, play referee to sibling fights, and make everyone happy. Often out of the goodness of our hearts, we assume a role we weren't assigned: the role of Savior. After a long day of striving to be and do it all, we realize the truth — it's tiring to play God.

"I can fix this" is a subtle lie, but make no mistake of its danger. It dethrones the only One who can truly help us — a Savior who doesn't grow weary and doesn't need eight hours of sleep.

In Psalm 28:7, David relied heavily on the Lord in times of trouble: "*The LORD is my strength and my shield; My heart trusted in Him, and I am helped; Therefore my heart greatly rejoices, And with my song I will praise Him.*" David declared God was his strength. He allowed his heart to trust in God, and the result was rejoicing.

When we recognize God as our strength and shield, we can let go of the torture of feeling responsible to solve everyone's problems. If God is big enough for you, then He is big enough for your family members and all their problems combined.

Before our problems are solved and the battle is won, victory starts with the reassignment of roles. We pray. The Lord protects. We trust. The Lord triumphs.

That afternoon, I embraced my daughter. My heart desperately wanted to fix all her problems with my words, but then I remembered who her Savior is. With eyes closed, I whispered to God, *Lord, be her strength. Be her shield.*

God knows the ache of our hearts, and He sees the hurt and pain in our families. When we purposefully turn our hearts to trust in Him as our family's "Fixer" and Savior, His strength creates beautiful space for our minds to rest in His care.

Let's relinquish the idea that everyone's happiness and welfare is up to us — because God didn't call us to be everyone's fixer. Instead, He wants us to call upon Him in times of trouble and trust in Him. In the atmosphere of trust, God helps us, and our hearts can rejoice.

Lord, I have put so much weight on myself to be the glue for my family and fix all their problems. I surrender my heart and emotions to You. I call upon You to be my family's strength and shield, and I ask You to help and heal each of my family members in the way You know is best. Hold us in Your might and power, and shield us from harm. I trust in You, and my heart rejoices. In Jesus' Name, Amen.

Quieting the Thief of Contentment

KELSEY CHADWICK

"When Peter saw him, he said to Jesus, 'Lord, what about this man?'"
John 21:21 (ESV)

The bright sun poured into my office, creating streams of warm light on my desk. Thankful for my window and a moment alone, I pulled out a turkey sandwich and my phone to enjoy a break from the day.

Suddenly, pictures of backyard sprinklers and purple popsicles at noon on a Tuesday flooded my screen as a friend gushed that she couldn't imagine having to work away from her kids this summer. My stomach dropped. I looked down at my sad lunch and imagined my kids eating chicken nuggets in front of the TV with the babysitter — again — waiting for me to pick them up.

Even though my family's choices had been bathed in prayer and I was confident I was where I needed to be that weekday afternoon, the enemy's lie that my friend had taken the better path started to take hold in my mind — daring me to doubt what God had said.

The Bible tells us that Jesus' first disciples struggled with comparison too. After Jesus was resurrected, He met with Peter to give him direction for the future. Soon, Jesus would return to heaven, but He had work for Peter to do. Three times, Jesus told him to build up His Church and disciple His followers. He even foretold that Peter would die for his faith (John 21:15-19). After having this pivotal encounter, Peter immediately saw his fellow apostle John and wondered what the Lord had for him.

"When Peter saw [John], he said to Jesus, 'Lord, what about this man?'"
(John 21:21).

On our best days, we want to know what is going on in each other's lives. But on our worst days, we compare our ideas and experiences to convince others (and maybe ourselves) that our choices are best.

Home-schooling vs. private schooling vs. public schooling …
Mom staying home vs. working outside the home …
Organic vegetables vs. a box of mac and cheese …

Maybe you have had a painful interaction around one of these topics that left you feeling less-than. I admit I have often found myself there — sometimes touting the freedom God has offered me but with an air of judgment toward those who have chosen something different, and sometimes giving into jealousy over the paths God has given to others.

Oh, friend, the lies of comparison dishonor what God has specifically designed for each of us — and we don't want to miss out on His best. We can rest in knowing that what He gives is for our good and His glory.

Father, You guide each of us uniquely and give us the freedom to take different roads. You use the diversity of people, places and things to reach the world for Yourself. Lord, help me follow You — and You alone. When I see others and wonder if their path is better, settle my gaze on You in faith that You know me better than I know myself. I trust You. In Jesus' Name, Amen.

We'll Never Be "Good Enough" for the Wrong Opportunities

MICHELLE MARTINO

"For am I now seeking the approval of man, or of God? Or am I trying to please man? If I were still trying to please man, I would not be a servant of Christ." Galatians 1:10 (ESV)

I fell back in my chair, staring blankly at the flickering light of my laptop. A discouraging message had appeared at the top of my inbox. As I scanned through the note, my head became heavy, and my body grew numb.

A job I applied for went to someone else. The actual message was filled with good wishes and encouraging feedback. I, however, wallowed in words of defeat: Inadequate. Worthless. Failure.

For my whole life, I had tried to avoid situations that could end in a potential letdown. Whenever I faced a challenge, I overworked myself to prove my worth to others. There was no room for risk, only a guarantee that I would never face rejection.

Now my faith floundered as I processed this career disappointment. *Why would God allow this to happen? Why wasn't I enough?* As I tried to make sense of the situation, God showed me that my desire to earn favor from people outweighed my intentions to serve Him.

In Galatians 1:10, Paul preaches that we cannot compromise who we serve: *"For am I now seeking the approval of man, or of God? Or am I trying to please man? If I were still trying to please man, I would not be a servant of Christ."* Misaligned motives lead to divided devotion.

We must be clear with our intentions if we are going to honor God. We must ask ourselves the same question before committing to a task: Will we strive for others' approval or live from the acceptance we already have in Christ? Through prayer, God brought me to a deeper level of awareness and developed in me a stronger conviction in this area.

My fear and discouragement about not being "good enough" stemmed from an insecure identity. To remember my worth, I took hold of scriptural truths:

- In Christ, I am chosen (John 15:16).
- I am not abandoned (Isaiah 41:10).
- I am loved (Romans 8:38-39).
- I have a hope and a future (Jeremiah 29:11).
- I am safe (Proverbs 29:25).
- I am always good enough because His grace covers me (2 Corinthians 12:9-10).

Any time I feel inferior, I declare these verses and pray them over my life. Instead of seeking recognition from people, I rest in the presence of a God who sees, knows and loves me.

Friend, we can stop questioning our value. We can overcome overthinking. No matter what people say, think or do, God has already accepted us. We'll never be "good enough" for the wrong opportunities. We can praise God for closed doors because His ways are better. He is the perfect door, the right path, and the only way for us.

Our human hearts may seek others' affection, but when we give God our full attention, we find that we are good enough for Him.

Heavenly Father, thank You for choosing me. No matter what I do, Your love and acceptance of me never change. Today I reject the lie that I am not enough. Help me to receive Your grace because where I am weak, You make me strong. My heart overflows with gratitude for who You are and how You see me. I want to honor You with my whole heart. In Jesus' Name, Amen.

Access Your Source of Confidence

TIFFANY WALKER

"for God gave us a spirit not of fear but of power and love and self-control." 2 Timothy 1:7 (ESV)

I enjoy going to the beach, but I am irrationally afraid of fish. I don't want anything to touch me without permission. I'm unable to pinpoint the source of the fear because I can't remember any traumatic aquatic experiences. The fear has always been there.

Once, when I was around 5, my mom told me the beach we were visiting didn't have fish. She said the water was too clear, so they avoided the area. This new information gave me a freedom I'd never felt before. I was riding waves, splashing and having a blast.

It's sad that fear can hinder us from doing a lot of things: getting in the water, calling a friend, or even sharing our story to help someone else get to know Jesus. We can start to believe the lies attached to the fear telling us we are weak, unloved or hopeless — making us less likely to step out of our comfort zone.

In 2 Timothy 1:7, the Apostle Paul was reminding Timothy that he shouldn't be afraid to spread the gospel because God hasn't given us a spirit of fear. He then pointed out three traits we have available as followers of Christ to overcome fear-induced lies.

1. We have power. The enemy wants us to believe we are weak, but because of Christ dwelling within us, we have access to His power (Romans 8:11). When we feel powerless in a situation, we can call upon His name and have authority to overcome.

2. We are loved. Do you ever feel lonely and isolated? Do you wonder if God even cares anymore? Isaiah 54:10 reminds us that His love will never leave us, even in the worst circumstances. God also loved us enough to send His Son as a sacrifice for our sins (1 John 4:9-11).

3. We have self-control. Maybe you've made some mistakes in the past that the enemy wants to keep bringing up. You feel defeated, not sure if you'll ever break free from destructive choices. But God's Word reminds us He will always provide a way out of sin (1 Corinthians 10:13). We just have to make sure we keep our eyes open. We don't have to give in to impulsivity when we have the Holy Spirit to guide our decisions.

My mom had the best of intentions that day on the beach. She saw how my fear was hindering me from enjoying life. Unfortunately, when I saw a boy running with a fish in his net, my fun came to an abrupt end.

I picture God looking at us with the same compassion my mom had for me. He doesn't want us paralyzed by our fear, so He uses *His Truth* to show us His power. Following His will can be scary, but He has given us all we need to defeat the lies of the enemy and wade into the unknown waters.

Lord, as I face today, I release my fears back to You. Please remind me that I am equipped with Your power, a power that can overcome the lies of the enemy. Help me to listen to Your voice speaking truth into my life. I know Your love will never leave me. I don't have to be afraid anymore. In Jesus' Name, Amen.

Overthinking Is Under-Trusting

CHRIS BAXTER

"Blessed is the man who trusts in the LORD, whose trust is the LORD."
Jeremiah 17:7 (ESV)

Overthinking is under-trusting. This phrase came to me in the wee hours of the morning as I was tossing and turning over a huge problem in my life. Ironically, I now don't even remember the reason for my fretting. At the time, however, I was all twisted up, both in my bedcovers and in my mind as I took turns playing the "should I or shouldn't I" and "what-if" mind games.

I'm not only the queen of second-guessing; I'm the queen of 222nd-guessing.

When I toss and turn, I'm like that double-minded individual mentioned in James, who asks for wisdom but doubts they will receive it: *"For that person must not suppose that he will receive anything from the Lord; he is a double-minded man, unstable in all his ways"* (James 1:7-8, ESV).

What is the remedy to these mental wrestling matches? Here are three thoughts that help me remember where to turn:

1. Choose to trust God's promises.
It's one thing to know God's promises, but it's another thing to *believe* them. In times of confusion, will I cling to God's Truth, or will I hold on to my fabrications? Questions such as *What if I'm making a mistake in this decision?* or *Did I really hear from God?* can be replaced with promises such as *"I will instruct you and teach you in the way you should go; I will counsel you with my eye upon you"* (Psalm 32:8, ESV). In this verse alone, God is promising to *instruct* us … *teach* us … *counsel* us. So instead of twirling with anxiety, I can repeatedly thank Him for these promises and then walk confidently by faith in His leading.

2. Choose to trust God's Spirit.

I tend to overthink the Holy Spirit. Sadly, this fleshly pause can lead to complete withdrawal from prayer or from listening for the Spirit's guidance. Yet when God's whisper enters my heart, nudging me to do His will, the truth is that I can either press forward in faith or shrink back in fear. Even if I "mishear" God, can I not trust my Good Shepherd enough to lead me back onto His right path? Certainly! He is *that good*. I must remember God looks for a faith-filled heart rather than flawless steps.

3. Choose to trust wise friends and mentors.

These carefully selected people can help confirm God's Truth in my life. Sharing my thoughts with those who will listen, encourage, advise and pray is a built-in blessing from God. He knows we need each other!

With these things in place, we can begin to say "no" to overthinking! Instead of tossing and turning with needless mind games, we can fully trust our God. "*Blessed is the man who trusts in the* LORD, *whose trust is the* LORD" (Jeremiah 17:7).

It's time for me to follow God's lead without hesitation. Will you join me? We've got Kingdom work to do — no doubt about it.

Dear heavenly Father, thank You for Your living Word and Your abiding Spirit. Thank You for the wise friends and mentors You have placed in my life. In times of overthinking, help me to recall Your truths and trust Your voice. Keep my heart in line with Yours, and make my footsteps firm. I want to move forward in faith every single day, confidently living for You. In Jesus' Name, Amen.

The Cost and Gain of Looking Back

KELLY SHANK

"Remember not the former things, nor consider the things of old. Behold, I am doing a new thing; now it springs forth, do you not perceive it? I will make a way in the wilderness and rivers in the desert." Isaiah 43:18-19 (ESV)

Three years ago, my son was diagnosed with autism spectrum disorder. I remember having two different feelings: deep thankfulness and a pit in my stomach so deep I thought I might get sick.

How does what enters our minds cause two such extreme responses? I have learned and am still learning that my response to any given situation is within my control. It is simply a matter of who I give my thoughts to.

Every thought I allow, every conversation I have and every choice I make will either reflect Christ or it won't. Many days, I allow Satan to play me like a fiddle.

I should have seen this coming.
If only I had noticed these signs sooner.
If only I had (fill in the blank).
Everything is my fault.

None of these thoughts I ponder ever draw me closer to the Lord. They never bring peace or joy; they aren't even true. Yet they can be so defeating.

In reading Genesis 19, we learn a lesson about leaving behind the negativity of the past. It features two cities, Sodom and Gomorrah, that were perverse and doomed for destruction. When the day arrived for the cities to be destroyed, God spared Lot and his family to fulfill a promise He made to Abraham, Lot's uncle. As Lot and his family were escaping the burning sulfur raining down on these two cities, two angels from God told them to flee and not look back: *"But Lot's wife, behind him, looked back, and she became a pillar of salt"* (Genesis 19:26, ESV).

I can relate to Lot's wife. I look back on things and allow them to harden me like a pillar of salt, only my hardening is from the inside out. It's gradual. But there's beauty in that slow hardening because that means there's time.

There is time to change my patterns of who I give my thoughts over to — time to have a different perspective. The prophet Isaiah gives us wisdom on how to consider the past: *"Remember not the former things, nor consider the things of old. Behold, [God is] doing a new thing; now it springs forth, do you not perceive it? [He] will make a way in the wilderness and rivers in the desert"* (Isaiah 43:18-19).

By God's gracious gift of time, I have been able to look at my son's autism diagnosis with a sense of thanksgiving because of all God has provided despite some hard struggles. I must actively replace the negative thoughts with positive ones.

There are times God wants us to look back — but not with a divided heart. He wants us to look back remembering that He was good even when our circumstances weren't. He wants us to remember His provision and His promises and then strain forward to what lies ahead because He is our prize (Philippians 3:13-14).

Dear Jesus, thank You for Your gift of grace. Thank You for providing a way out of the negative thoughts that can so easily entangle me. Thank You for never leaving my side. Help me to boldly run this race You've set before me — with a thankful heart because I'm running toward You. I love You. In Jesus' Name, Amen.

Where You'll Find Comfort

ANGEL VARNEY

"Keep me as the apple of your eye; hide me in the shadow of your wings ..."
Psalm 17:8 (ESV)

Unstructured time is a treasured delight of summer around our house. Bedtimes tend to fly out the window, and my teens will open up their hearts wider as the sun fades away. I hold that time dear as I peer into the parts of their lives they share more vulnerably in the lamplight of the evening.

With sharing comes revelation, though, and that revelation can lead to worries. Worries can lead to sleepless nights. Such was the case one recent evening, and as morning finally dawned, I was glad to see the sunrise and open the day with God's Word.

My daily reading took me to Psalm 17:8: "*Keep me as the apple of your eye; hide me in the shadow of your wings ...*"

As this psalm was written, David had likely been on the run from his enemy Saul for years, hiding in caves and dodging arrows. Saul's pursuit of David must have felt exhausting. Right in the middle of God's perfect will, we read so clearly that David was tired, weary and worried as he poured out his heart to God.

Life for us today as 21st-century Christians can also feel worrisome and exhausting. We will often face hardships that are too heavy to carry on our own. The good news is that just as David didn't fight his battles alone, we aren't meant to rely on our own strength for today's challenges either. Our comfort is found in the shadow of God's wings.

As a mother bird pulls her chicks close under her feathers to care for and protect them, so our Lord desires to pull us close and comfort us as well. There, under His wings, we can rest in His embrace and feel the covering of His faithfulness. There, the battle with worry is won as we surrender our problems to His sovereign provision.

David knew God so intimately that even in the midst of trouble, assured that he was the apple of God's eye, David was hidden from harm in the shadow of God's wings.

Perhaps we, too, can learn from David and gather up every concern and every worry that keeps us awake at night, then run to our heavenly Father's covering for shelter. May our concerns draw us ever closer to the Father in intimacy as we surrender our burdens to Him.

Heavenly Father, I give the worries and concerns of this day to You right now. Help me to remember, like David did, that I am the apple of Your eye. No problem of mine is too small or too big for You. You see and care for every concern. Help me to rest in Your embrace as I surrender and there feel the heartbeat of who You are instead of feeling any worry that plagues my mind. In Jesus' Name, Amen.

What's the Alternative?

PAM WINKE

"Guide me in your truth and teach me, for you are God my Savior, and my hope is in you all day long." Psalm 25:5 (NIV)

"But what's the alternative?"

The question seemed reasonable as I sat with a couple of my small-group friends and we contrasted God's unchangeability with our personal need to grow and change.

As soon as I asked it, my mind raced back to a season over 20 years ago when my mom had called and asked me the same thing. I was right in the middle of what had already been an hour-long effort to dress my infant son and 2-year-old daughter, stock a travel bag, get out the door, get to the gym, and justify the membership I just bought.

She could sense the stress in my voice and calmly asked, "What's the alternative, honey?"

After her phone call, I considered what she had said ... I could either cave to my feelings of fatigue and frustration and never leave the house until the kids were grown or I could accept this temporary stage of motherhood, load the kids in the car, and pursue some much-needed self-care. Clearly, the choice was mine.

I didn't realize it at the time, but the question of alternatives has been a guiding question of wisdom throughout my life. Daily life offers every one of us untold opportunities to believe, embrace, claim and exercise God's promises of provision offered in the Truth of His Word ... or not.

The alternative is to live doubtful, paralyzed and powerless in fear. That's not how I want to live, but when I allow the deceiver or any other outside force to have a louder voice in my head than my Savior does, I set myself up for defeat. That's when I need to remember that God is faithful and that His Word is the reassuring hope I need.

As believers in Christ, we have the Holy Spirit as our constant companion and *source* of Truth who will guide us *into* all Truth (John 16:13). But first we must consciously choose to listen to and hope in His voice. Psalm 25:5 shows us how to pray for this: "*Guide me in your truth and teach me, for you are God my Savior, and my hope is in you all day long.*"

As my friends and I further discussed God's divine attribute of immutability that day, we also pondered the alternative: believing that our *circumstances* were immutable and would never change. In truth, almost nothing in life is static, the clock never stops ticking, and life does go on. Looking at my now-20-something son and daughter testifies to that.

No matter what alternatives present themselves, let's always choose to live Holy Spirit-power-filled lives fueled by God's Word.

Dear heavenly Father, please help still my soul in order to hear Your voice amid the chaos. Please help me walk in the power of the Holy Spirit, who is my advocate and constant companion. Give me wisdom to choose Your life-affirming Truth versus self-defeating lies. And when I am tired, stressed or anxious for tomorrow, remind me that Your Word will be my guide forward, one lamp-lit step at a time. In Jesus' Name, Amen.

Replacing Worst-Case-Scenario Thinking

MARY FOLKERTS

"Finally, brothers and sisters, whatever is true, whatever is noble, whatever is right, whatever is pure, whatever is lovely, whatever is admirable—if anything is excellent or praiseworthy—think about such things."
Philippians 4:8 (NIV)

I sat gazing out the picture window, my eyes fixed on the road, my stomach tied in knots. My young mind raced with all the bad things that could have potentially happened to my parents, who were late coming home from a trip. My parents did eventually arrive, but not before I had allowed my thoughts to create intense anxiety within me.

I was an anxious child, and the anxiety didn't settle down as I got older. In fact, it increased as my imagination grew, and the thoughts circling my mind became vines determined to choke the joy right out of my heart.

If a thought came to me, I believed it had a valid reason to be there. Even though it frightened and depressed me, I would rehearse it as if to lessen its impact on my heart. It didn't work. Letting my mind wander unchecked only created high anxiety and fear. I set up camp in a town called Worst-Case Scenario — and then wondered why I worried so much.

Years later, it was my sister, who had been diagnosed with an early form of breast cancer, who taught me I didn't have to entertain every thought that slithered into my mind. She spoke the words over the telephone, and they hit differently this time: "Think about the things that are true, right, pure and lovely," she said. These ideas from Philippians 4:8 were the things she had to tell herself time and again when she imagined her children without a mother.

There is a good reason why God's Word instructs us to be careful with our thoughts. We are not to be lazy about what we think; instead, we must take our thoughts captive (2 Corinthians 10:5) as though we are fighting in a battle, which, indeed, we are. It's a battle for our minds and our souls! The enemy wants nothing more than to make us weak-minded, anxious and gullible to every lie he throws our way! Because if we believe the lie long enough, it will become our truth.

How can we stop the swirling lies?

1. When a thought enters our minds, we can ask ourselves: *Is it true? Is it pure and lovely? Praiseworthy and uplifting?* If not, stop! Fight back with a Bible verse, or turn up the worship music, anything to interrupt the trajectory of the unwanted thought.

2. Do it again. And again. This is key to our struggle against the lies that determine to destroy us. Each time we are confronted with thoughts that bring us anxiety, we must chase them to the only One who can change our thinking patterns: Jesus.

The more we interrupt our negative thought patterns with God's Truth, the less often negativity will be our primary response to life.

Dear Jesus, You speak Truth! Help me fight this battle for my mind! Remind me to take each thought captive, silencing the negativity that tries to claim me. You are not the author of fear! Let me soak in the Truth of Your Word, and teach me to recognize the thoughts that are lies. Help me to spend more time praising You for who You are and all You have provided and to spend less time ruminating on all the things that cause me to fear. In Jesus' Name, Amen.

Anchored in Hope

AMELIA SMITH

"We have this as a sure and steadfast anchor of the soul, a hope that enters into the inner place behind the curtain, where Jesus has gone as a forerunner on our behalf …" Hebrews 6:19-20 (ESV)

Growing up around the seashore, I was fascinated by how the sea changed yet stayed the same. In the car with my mother, we once passed over the sound as I counted the boats in the small harbor. The clouds quickly became dark, and the once calm waters were now teeming with busy boatmen throwing out additional anchors.

"Why do they do that, Mother?" I asked.

She explained that when storms arise, the boatmen pitch out at least one additional anchor to steady their boats on the bow and the stern. Otherwise, with only one anchor, the boats would spin with the increasing wind, possibly causing them to flip and sink.

Storms come to us all. At times, in my blended family of six adult children, their spouses and nine grandchildren, I have felt utterly unmoored by the storms we are facing. You can imagine our lives are fulfilling yet occasionally riddled with challenges. Yet God in His mercy has shown me how to anchor my faith in Him and not in my desired outcome.

Walking through storms in my life, I've learned that I have two anchors: the character of God and the Word of God. In Hebrews 6:18 we see two characteristics of God we can hold on to: 1) He does not lie and 2) His promises are sure. He reaches into our mess as He draws near to the brokenhearted. Our hope is sure.

In storms, my reactions reveal what's in my heart. When fears assail me, I ask the Lord: *What is the lie I'm believing, and what is the truth from Your Word that I can use against this lie?* Usually, the lie is that I must control my outcome. What's driving my need for control is fear. The truth is that I can trust that God is at work in my circumstances, and I can rest in His sovereign rule.

I keep Bible verses written on index cards in my purse as a ready weapon to unleash against the enemy when I'm tempted to give in to the lies swirling around in my head.

Today, don't let the enemy of your soul shipwreck your faith. You have *"a sure and steadfast anchor of the soul,"* and His name is Jesus (Hebrews 6:19). In Hebrews 6:20, we see that *"Jesus has gone as a forerunner on our behalf."* Jesus paid the penalty of the death we deserved so that we might have life. The life Jesus offers is abundant — not free from storms but rich in hope as we surrender ourselves to Him.

Dear Jesus, I am sinking, weighted down with the storms in my life. I am weary and worn. You know my struggles: fear, control, guilt, shame. With open hands, Lord, I surrender. Thank You that You are near to me even now, even in my mess. You are my anchor, my hope. I place my trust in You and in Your Word. In Jesus' Name, Amen.

I Will Be Hopeful and Joyful — Even if Life Turns Upside Down

SHARON KERN MCCALL

"yet I will rejoice in the Lord; I will take joy in the God of my salvation."
Habakkuk 3:18 (ESV)

My mom baked pineapple upside-down cakes. Each ingredient and step of her trusted recipe was necessary. After beating the batter, she poured it over the chosen ingredients placed at the bottom of the pan. These goodies were hidden in the heat of the dark oven. The fragrance filled the house and increased our anticipation as we waited.

At the appointed time, a seemingly simple cake was removed from the pan — simple until carefully flipped over to reveal a luscious cake with pineapples, cherries and nuts on the top. It wasn't a mistake for the cake to go through this process in the oven. It was always intended to be flipped right-side up.

We may think we're beaten when we go through dark, heated and upside-down seasons of despair. We can easily identify times when life turned upside down because of reckless decisions, death, divorce, shame, infertility, wayward children, health issues and other challenges. We may even question God about His purpose.

In these seasons, how do we prevent negative thoughts from taking up residence in our minds and defeating us? We find the answer in Habakkuk's extended dialogue with God.

With frustration, the prophet Habakkuk questioned God about his upside-down situation. He lamented the injustice, evil and tragedy the people of Israel's southern kingdom endured under the captivity of the Babylonians. Why hadn't God stepped in to deliver them?

Habakkuk questioned God's inaction, and he expected answers. He cried out to ask *"how long"* and *"why"* (Habakkuk 1:2-3, ESV).

The Lord replied that He was the One who had raised up the Babylonians (Habakkuk 1:5-11).

Habakkuk cried out to ask why God would use this wicked nation (Habakkuk 1:12-17).

God instructed Habakkuk to write down a promise of judgment for Babylon at an appointed time. God gave him assurance: *"If it seems slow, wait for it; it will surely come ..."* (Habakkuk 2:3, ESV).

The third chapter of Habakkuk is about renewed hope. While still in captivity, Habakkuk progressed from a frustrated conversation to a joyful prayer of praise. He concluded with these "I will" statements: *"Yet I will rejoice in the Lord; I will take joy in the God of my salvation"* (Habakkuk 3:18).

God is glorified by our praise even if our prayers seem unanswered, the circumstances remain unchanged and deliverance isn't apparent. While we wait on Him, we can take our thoughts captive (2 Corinthians 10:5) and rely on Christ with heartfelt worship during the heat of dark and uncertain seasons.

Like Habakkuk, I will delight in the Lord with a mindset of hope despite upside-down situations. I will trust His proven recipe and His plan, knowing Christ has an appointed time to flip things right-side up.

For now, I will make a choice to rejoice — not only about what God does but about who He is.

Heavenly Father, I worship and glorify You for who You are. Thank You for salvation through Christ. Please forgive me for my shortcomings as I struggle with the upside-down frustrations of life. Please renew my mind, and help me release my unanswered questions to You and trust Your Word, guidance and timing. Even if I don't see a resolution, I will rejoice, and I will stand on Your Word and Your recipe for my life. In Jesus' Name, Amen.

The Thread of God's Faithful Love

JUDITH LAPP

"For I am convinced that neither death nor life, neither angels nor demons, neither the present nor the future, nor any powers, neither height nor depth, nor anything else in all creation, will be able to separate us from the love of God that is in Christ Jesus our Lord." Romans 8:38-39 (NIV)

Another day dawns, clear and bright, with all the minutes and seconds untainted and stretched before me. I step into the day with confidence and the assurance of who I am in my Father. I'm ready and armed with God's new morning mercies, His provision of grace. I know He loves me.

But then.

I forget to write that text. A friend feels missed. Relationships go awry. And expectations aren't met. In the midst of the daily minutes of my day, I struggle to rest in God as my fears and shortcomings escalate.

These rhythms soon weave their tendrils of doubt and mistrust around my heart and cause me to question the goodness of God when just a bit ago I was so very sure.

With these rhythms come thought threads that invade my mind and heart:

> *I messed up.*
> *I'm too much and yet not enough.*
> *I'm not worth anything.*
> *I'm a disappointment.*

Satan keeps building his web of lies and partial truths, and in my weariness, I get a bit lost in the weaving. I struggle and fight to remember the greater Truth of God, but then I begin to question if He really is for me … just like Eve did so many years ago in the garden of Eden (Genesis 3).

And like Eve, I reach. I reach for managing on my own, thinking, *I'll just do it myself.* Or I succumb to the fear of the unknown, anxiety bogs me down, and my heart wrestles. Then the words of Scripture come quietly and surely alongside the tumultuous thoughts, and they remind me with a whisper that God's love never ceases.

So I stop. I pause to remember another thread, another weaving of words.

If God so loved me yesterday, and He doesn't change, then today His love is still the same. It is still here. And tucked in throughout the Scriptures are words of God declaring His goodness, faithfulness and love. His thread of faithful love.

His greater Truth reminds us of the reality of His unfailing love and will ground our hearts in the midst of the stormy thoughts:

"For I am convinced that neither death nor life, neither angels nor demons, neither the present nor the future, nor any powers, neither height nor depth, nor anything else in all creation, will be able to separate us from the love of God that is in Christ Jesus our Lord" (Romans 8:38-39).

Nothing. *Nothing* shall separate us from the love of God. So, dear friends, that means nothing changes God's love. He is who He is, and what you or I do won't change it. The truest thing about us is that we are faithfully loved by Him — no matter what.

Father, open the eyes of my heart to see You today. Help me to pause, and grant me the courage to stay with You. Grant me the courage to believe Your greater Truth and receive the grace You so graciously provide every new morning. Thank You. Thank You for Your faithful love, the thread that holds each day and every happening together to weave a tapestry that only You can create. I pray these things with love and gratefulness. In Jesus' Name, Amen.

From Disappointment to Discovery: The Power of Pausing

KIM MCGOVERN

"Trust in the Lord *with all your heart and lean not on your own understanding; in all your ways submit to him, and he will make your paths straight." Proverbs 3:5-6 (NIV)*

I clenched my phone as I waited for a reply. *Did she keep her promise? I'm sure she followed through. Yet I haven't heard from her all weekend.*

Ding!

It wasn't the reply I expected. Instead of relief, I found myself engulfed in disappointment — again.

Why didn't she let me know she couldn't keep her promise? Didn't she understand how important this was? How could she be so thoughtless?

The blinking cursor begged for my response. Reacting while irritated would only lead to trouble.

Pause.

Setting my phone facedown on the dining table, I took a deep breath. What had once felt like an impossible-to-obey nudge from God was evolving into a rhythm of restoration in my life — one I relished when emotions threatened to overwhelm me. Pausing allowed me to have time to process the situation without overreacting.

I needed to understand the root of my offended feelings to halt the impending downpour of negativity in my head. It would take God's insight into the situation and His promise of a straight path to lead me out. Proverbs 3:5-6 says it this way: *"Trust in the* Lord *with all your heart and lean not on your own understanding; in all your ways submit to him, and he will make your paths straight."*

Wrestling with negative thoughts and emotions is a daily battle. Have you ever wondered what to do when they threaten to steal your joy and peace? In these moments, why not practice taking a pause?

❧ **Pausing gives us an opportunity to get curious about our thoughts.** Curiosity is vital to capturing chaotic thoughts and emotions and submitting them to God for transformation.

❧ **Pausing provides us with a moment to pray for wisdom.** Prayer invites God into the discovery process, allowing Him to help unearth the origins of the negativity.

❧ **Pausing allows us space to embrace God's Truth.** Processing insights about our thoughts and feelings in light of God's Word enables His Truth to reshape ill-conceived thinking.

❧ **Pausing offers us a chance to preach to our hearts.** Speaking God's Truth to unfavorable thoughts and emotions reminds us of who God is and who we are in Christ, transforming us in the process.

❧ **Pausing gives us an occasion to praise God for His faithfulness.** Even during challenging circumstances, God's faithfulness provides reasons to praise Him. By focusing on His goodness, we can shift our perspective from dissatisfaction to gratitude.

Wondering about that blinking cursor? Pausing opened the way for God, through His wisdom, to remold my complaints into a compassionate response toward the person on the other end of the phone.

Next time you're tempted to ruminate in the wrong direction, consider taking a pause instead. Let curiosity capture negative thoughts, uncover their roots, and transform them with the truths of God's promises.

Lord, I'm raw and weary, overwhelmed with thoughts and feelings that won't let go. I give them all to You and ask You to transform them with Your Truth. Soften my resistant heart with Your compassion, and show me a way back to peace so I might forgive others as You always forgive me. You promise wisdom to all who ask for it. Please help me understand the root of the disappointment dragging me down. Help me find rest in You and experience Your joy. In Jesus' Name, Amen.

Using the Armor God Gave You

MICHELLE SNIPPE

"Take the helmet of salvation and the sword of the Spirit, which is the word of God." Ephesians 6:17 (NIV)

I couldn't find my shoes. The comfy ones I wear every single day.

I rummaged through the closet, moving sandals and runners and grocery store bags, none of which were where they belonged. Honestly, the closet was a mess, and it was frustrating my search, which was turning up nothing.

But while tossing footwear this way and that, what *did* turn up was a voice rising within telling me that because my closet was a mess, my entire life must be too. With that thought, my mind was further coerced into a pit full of condemning chatter.

You know that Bible study you went to last week? You talked too much. That project you're working on for the church? You're not qualified for that. How can you be so disorganized all the time? Your family wishes you'd just get your act together.

The voice shouted these and many other accusations at me for the full three-minute shoe search.

Are you aware of how many shaming lies you can heap upon yourself in three minutes? How many past faults you can dig up in 180 seconds? *A lot.*

And it all started because I was looking for a pair of shoes.

You know, the enemy is crafty. And he's been honing his "skills" for thousands of years, studying just when and where to aim his arrows. As a result, his deployment is stellar. And it seems, on certain days, it's easy to cave to his marksmanship.

But in those moments of spiraling, we must stop.

Stop shaming ourselves with lies.
Stop rehearsing our perceived failures.

Stop focusing on the arrows and start *fighting* them.

But how does one fend off all the fiery falsehoods that threaten to burn a hole in our hearts?

The Bible tells us: **with a sword.**

The Apostle Paul writes in Ephesians 6:17, "*Take the helmet of salvation and the sword of the Spirit, which is the word of God.*"

This piece of God's armor is full of power and truth designed to equip our minds for defense in spiritual battle. Alongside our shield of faith, it forms a strong weapon to extinguish the flaming darts the devil fires our way, preventing them from making their mark.

By the power of the Word, we proclaim the truth. Solid truth. And we shout that truth against the lies.

I am not alone.
I am not condemned.
I am forgiven and loved.
I am of great value to God.
I am fearfully and wonderfully made.

If your mind is spinning with lies right now or the assaulting arrows are relentless, please know this: You have a weapon. A sword, which is the Word of God.

So let's read it. Memorize it. Meditate on it. Believe it. Renew our minds with it. And take the hand God offers to pull us up, out and onto higher ground.

Loving Father, I feel like the enemy is trying to get the best of me right now. His arrows of lies are aimed at me, and he's letting them fly. But, Father, I know that Your Word is my weapon. It is filled with truth that thwarts the lies. Help me to renew my mind with Scripture, all for Your honor and glory. In Jesus' Name, Amen.

Our Past Is Meant To Stay in the Past

TRACI SHNIDER

"… but I focus on this one thing: Forgetting the past and looking forward to what lies ahead, I press on to reach the end of the race and receive the heavenly prize for which God, through Christ Jesus, is calling us." Philippians 3:13-14 (NLT)

I tossed and turned as I reflected on the mistakes of my past. *You're never going to find your purpose in the Kingdom of God. You've done too much.* Rolling over, I drew the blanket tightly around me, trying to shut out the persistent whispers in my head.

Tears fell silently as I stared at the clock and watched time slowly tick by. *God, is my purpose within You being held hostage because of the things I've said, the things I've done? Please forgive me, Lord.*

The Holy Spirit met me in my guilt and shame. *My daughter, I have forgiven you. Any more guilt over these forgiven sins is from the enemy, not from Me.* I felt His inner peace, and as daylight peeked its head into my window, I finally fell asleep.

Maybe you feel this, too, as the enemy hits the "refresh" button over and over again on your past imperfections and failures. All too often, we define ourselves today based on the mistakes of our yesterdays, and it's an exhausting way to live.

But God doesn't want us dwelling on the past. He wants us to dwell on the redemption of Jesus. And that's why He inspired Paul to write this very truth in Philippians 3:13-14:

"But I focus on this one thing: Forgetting the past and looking forward to what lies ahead, I press on to reach the end of the race and receive the heavenly prize for which God, through Christ Jesus, is calling us."

Friend, our windshield is much bigger than our rearview mirror. And it's hard to press forward in this race for Christ if we're continually looking back at the regrets of our past.

If anyone's past could have paralyzed their purpose for Jesus, it would have been the Apostle Paul's. Before he was Paul, he was known as Saul, a great persecutor of the early Christians. He took part in the stoning of Stephen, a church leader (Acts 7:57-60). He wreaked havoc on the early Church by dragging men and women from their homes and throwing them into prison. And it was while he was on his way to persecute Christians in Damascus that Saul encountered Jesus, who changed his story forever (Acts 9). Now better known as Paul, this former persecutor became a soldier for Christ and wrote more than half of the New Testament.

It's highly unlikely our past parallels with Paul's. But if he could move beyond his past in his mission for Christ, why do we allow the enemy to paralyze us with our past? Our past is meant to stay right where it belongs — in our past.

Jesus brought down from heaven the sweet promise of redemption, and for those who believe in Him, our slate is wiped clean by His precious blood. So as you lay down your head tonight, don't buy the lie that because of your past mistakes, God is withholding what He has for you. Instead, dwell on the redemption of Jesus, know that you're forgiven, and keep running the race toward the heavenly prize He's set aside for you (Hebrews 12:1).

Dear heavenly Father, the enemy always seems to come knocking on the door of my mind at night. Help me to silence his haunting whispers, and lead me to Your peace. Please forgive me for dwelling on my past and allowing it to rob me of the purpose You have set before me. I choose to meditate on the truth of Your promises that I can rest in Your forgiveness. And help me, Lord, to begin my race again in the morning. In Jesus' Name, Amen.

Safety in Rough Waters

SANDRA YERIAN

"When you pass through the waters, I will be with you; and through the rivers, they shall not overwhelm you; when you walk through fire you shall not be burned, and the flame shall not consume you." Isaiah 43:2 (ESV)

I felt I was drowning in an ocean of anxiety. Fatigue and discouragement overwhelmed me. But it hadn't always been like that. Since being diagnosed with breast cancer in early spring, I'd been riding a wave of positivity.

God's hand was obviously guiding every step from that first suspicious finding to the present. My medical team, treatment plan and support network all came together in perfect timing. I rejoiced in God's goodness and was confident I'd emerge from this healthy once again. I was excited to share what God had done and was continuing to do in my life.

However, this was a long, exhausting journey. Even with such a positive prognosis, there were frequent complications and delays. Treatment seemed to stretch endlessly before me. The sparkling, positive energy began to falter, crowded out by stress and anxiety. Spiritually, I began to feel distant and alone.

But God is faithful, and He provided uplifting inspiration when I needed it most. One morning during my devotional time, I received the precious gift of these words from the prophet Isaiah:

"When you pass through the waters, I will be with you; and through the rivers, they shall not overwhelm you; when you walk through fire you shall not be burned, and the flame shall not consume you" (Isaiah 43:2).

The words spoke directly into my troubled mind.

When our lives present us with challenging circumstances, we may feel terribly lost and lonely. Yet the promises in Scripture are deeply comforting. God is with us as we navigate uncharted waters. He once parted the Red Sea to bring His chosen people, the fleeing Israelites, to safety (Exodus 14).

Our loving Father does the same for all His precious children today, making a way for us to reach eternal safety through faith in Jesus. We can hold on to this truth.

We cannot know the crises we will face in our lifetime. Confusion and distress threaten our peace. But by internalizing the words of Scripture, we can be confident our trials will not overwhelm us.

I love the story of the Apostle Peter walking on the water with Jesus. When Peter doubted and began to sink, Jesus grabbed his hand (Matthew 14:29-31). Jesus extends His saving grace to us as well. He will never let us sink under the weight of our fear. With the strength of His hand, He will hold us above the crashing waves.

Today, the treatments and surgery are behind me. Gratefully I rejoice that our gracious God brought me through this difficult season. I am resuming the normal rhythms of my life as a new creation transformed by the journey.

Dear friend, I don't know what painful, confusing reality has invaded your life, hijacking your peace, but I do know this: When we lean into the loving arms of Jesus, trusting Him completely, He will hold us securely, and we will find comfort and strength to endure.

Father, in Your Word, I find strength for the battles I face. Remind me always to lean into Your welcoming embrace when the challenges seem overwhelming. In You, I find courage to face each new day. Thank You for the gift of Your constant presence and especially for Your precious Son. In Jesus' Name, Amen.

The Power of Your Beliefs

LAUREN MITCHELL

"So we have come to know and to believe the love that God has for us."
1 John 4:16a (ESV)

Because I tend to talk with my hands and tell loud stories, I'm well suited for my job as a middle school teacher. One day as we were learning prepositions, which practically beg to be acted out, I learned an important truth that has stuck with me.

I had just finished describing "under the desk" and "around the classroom." Picture tons of motions and lots of laughter. I brought the class back to focus and assigned some practice work. No sooner had I gotten situated than a student asked a clarifying question. Of course needing motions to answer, I stood up and gave a great example. Everyone sighed in recognition, and then it happened.

You see, while "clarifying" the question (dancing around), I positioned myself just short of my chair. I firmly believed that my feet had remained planted for the duration of the illustration, but it wasn't true. I sat down, completely missing the chair, and in a blaze of glory crashed to the floor. You can imagine the reaction; there wasn't much more preposition learning after that.

I wholeheartedly believed my chair was right behind me, and that belief led to my actions, which led to the floor.

We all react the same way to a rubber snake we think is real as we would to a real snake. Our actions will flow from what we believe. Not just what we say we believe but what we actually believe. And that's not necessarily the truth of the situation.

I love how the Apostle John puts this truth so succinctly: *"So we have come to know and to believe the love that God has for us"* (1 John 4:16a). John knew and believed in Jesus, and that belief propelled John to a life fueled by faith. If we really know God, we will believe His love for us. If we believe His love for us, our actions will flow from security and purpose.

But we have to lead our thoughts to the truth on purpose. I love how Lamentations puts this: "'*My portion is the* L*ORD,' I have said to myself, so I will put my hope in him*" (Lamentations 3:24, NET). Sometimes leading my thoughts requires that I talk to myself. I have to tell myself the truth and encourage my heart to know and believe.

I can always look at my actions to decide what I am believing. So many of us never really examine the thoughts we are listening to. But we can learn to silence the lies that fuel our actions into anxiety, apathy, insecurity and disobedience. We can recognize when we are feeling anxious and insecure and then trace it back to our thoughts.

Jesus is the way, the truth and the life (John 14:6). Knowing Jesus opens the door to believing Jesus. Then we can lead our thoughts — and in turn, our actions — into purpose and joy instead of in circles of doubt and shame.

What or who are you believing?

Do your actions sync with your belief?

Father, open our eyes to our practiced beliefs because we don't always recognize how we are being led by them. Help us create new paths and patterns for our thoughts based on the truth about You that we come to know and then believe. Thank You that Your love for us can redefine every situation and decision. Help us take our thoughts captive to obey Christ. In Jesus' Name, Amen.

Three Powerful Words To Pray

CARRIE ROER

"I lift up my eyes to the hills. From where does my help come? My help comes from the LORD, who made heaven and earth." Psalm 121:1-2 (ESV)

It had been a day. You know, the kind where it seems like everything you touch falls apart and every conversation ends poorly. My mind had started to spiral faster and faster into deeper and deeper thoughts that my rational brain knew were lies whispered from the enemy … but my emotional brain believed them.

The devil is sneaky. He cannot create anything (that's God's job), but he can take a true statement or occurrence and twist it just enough to become a lie that seems truthful.

This particular day, some of the twists included these thoughts:

My kids aren't listening to what I'm asking them to do … therefore, I'm a bad mom.

My stomach hurts because I ate too much … therefore, I'll never become the healthiest version of myself. Why keep trying?

Something I said to a family member was misunderstood … therefore, no one cares about me.

I found myself in the shower, tears mixing with the water on my face, unable to form a rational (or even irrational) thought beyond the twisted lies … until three little words came out: *Help me, God.*

I repeated them over and over as I finished my shower, put on pajamas and sat on my bed. No answers came immediately, but my mind slowly began to clear, and my heart rate calmed. No Bible verses came to mind, and no other prayers were prayed. But I fell asleep in peace.

The writer of Psalm 121 knew where to look when he was in distress: *"I lift up my eyes to the hills. From where does my help come? My help comes from the LORD, who made heaven and earth"* (Psalm 121:1-2).

Why is it so easy to take our focus off God? He is our Creator, Helper, Savior and Healer. He is the One who knows us better than anyone else, the One who says He will answer when we call. Yet so often, when we stumble, our physical and spiritual eyes look down, and we focus on what's directly around us instead of on Him.

When we find ourselves flat on our faces, fighting to hear God's voice over the voice of the enemy, condemning ourselves because we should be better than this, the process it will take to get out of that pit can seem insurmountable. We're tired and cranky, and we just don't feel like fighting for it. It's too hard.

In those moments, just ask for help. *Help me, God* is a simple prayer acknowledging three things:

1. *Help* — I ask and expect Him to answer.
2. *Me* — I'm struggling.
3. *God* — I turn my focus solely to Him.

The next steps toward combating lies and renewing our minds will come in time. But first, let's lift our eyes off the floor and up to the hills, to the One who longs to hear His children ask for help. We can look away from ourselves, away from our circumstances, away from everything except Him. If we redirect our focus, the rest of the process will follow.

God, there are times in my life when I listen to the lies of the enemy instead of truths from You. It can be so hard to look up when I find myself down. When my mind starts to spiral, let Your Spirit nudge my heart to take the very first step toward peace — returning my focus to You and asking for Your help. Thank You for Your promises never to leave me and to listen when I call. In Jesus' Name, Amen.

Faith for Our Hardest Journeys

JOBY SALICETI

"You hem me in, behind and before, and lay your hand upon me." Psalm 139:5 (ESV)

My heart raced as I gripped the test instructions. My shoulders felt tight, my neck stiff. With a knotted stomach, I began reading the first questions of the end-of-year test to my youngest daughter — who sat waiting at her desk, sharpened No. 2 pencils by her side.

It was our day of reckoning. The testing would tell us how we were doing with our new home-schooling journey. The voice of doubt rang loudly in my ears, reminding me of my long list of inadequacies.

Fear of failure had gripped me throughout the year and tempted me to quit. I had no formal training. Why did I think I could do this? But the Lord repeatedly reminded me that He is with me: He "*hem[s] me in, behind and before, and lay[s His] hand upon me*" (Psalm 139:5).

David penned these words in a desperate time of trouble. A Hebrew word often used for "hem" (*tsuwr*) means to confine, secure, enclose or guard a valuable object. It gives the impression of protecting completely. By using this word, David acknowledged that we are important to God: He lovingly surrounds His people and protects us in the situations we face. He is there before we ever set foot on the path, and He is there long after we leave it.

God is by our side, even when the enemy wants to whisper — or scream — otherwise. It was true for David then, and, friend, it is true for us today.

I love the way this verse is paraphrased in The Message Bible: "*I look behind me and you're there, then up ahead and you're there, too—your reassuring presence, coming and going.*"

God cares tremendously for us. He wants to lead, protect and guide us. With Him by my side, why do I fear? Because I take my eyes off Him and His perfect faithfulness and instead fixate on my own failures.

Was the test the deciding factor of my success as a home-school educator or my daughter's as a student? Of course not. Faithfully following God and trusting Him to do what only He can do is more important than the outcome. This is where our faith flourishes. Having verses like this one tucked in my heart helps remind me of truth in times of trouble and squash the lies that the enemy speaks.

Thankfully, despite my shortcomings, my daughter finished the test with flying colors. And while that did bring relief to my weary soul, it was also one more moment to reflect on God's goodness.

He led us to this path. He hemmed us in. And He will see us through to the end.

This is the voice I am choosing to believe.

Father, I thank You that You hem me in. You are with me wherever I go and surround me in Your lovingkindness. Please help me silence the lies of the enemy. I pray that I will focus on Your presence in my path. Help me to know that You truly love me and are for me, and You are with me despite what the enemy says. Help the Truth of Your Word to be the voice that speaks loudest in my life. In Jesus' Name, Amen.

How To Find Rest and Renewal

JULIE LUBKEMAN SMITH

"Do not be anxious about anything, but in every situation, by prayer and petition, with thanksgiving, present your requests to God." Philippians 4:6 (NIV)

The alarm jangled loudly, yet I was already awake. Instantly, I could feel a blanket of heaviness over me. The thoughts were already churning in my head before my feet even hit the floor.

It doesn't matter what I do; nothing seems to work. I've failed my family because of it. What happened to the thriving woman I once was? I'm just not enough. God, why can't I hear You? This happened every morning for a long, hard season. I couldn't seem to turn off the anxious thoughts that made me feel this way.

But eventually I stopped trying to control every aspect of my life, and I surrendered. I decided not to fight this on my own anymore. I would trust God to show me what He wanted me to learn. My mind needed rest, and I discovered the only way to do that was to draw closer to the Father and allow Him to renew my mind (Romans 12:2).

Here are three practices that have helped me find renewal:

1. Rest. In adulthood, I had stopped connecting with God through nature. But to help my anxiety, I started walking outside again, every day. I would close my eyes and listen to the birds and the wind in the trees. I'd notice the brilliant colors around me. Focusing on God's creation with all my senses was highly effective at quieting those anxious thoughts. It was rest for my brain and my soul.

"… Whatever is pure, whatever is lovely, whatever is admirable— if anything is excellent or praiseworthy—think about such things" (Philippians 4:8, NIV).

2. Reframe. When I'd catch myself in a spiral of anxious thoughts, I would stop and ask myself, *Is it true?* If the answer was "no," I'd ask, *What does God say is true?* I chose to focus on that. I had to turn to Him and reframe my thoughts with God's Truth many times each day.

"... Whatever is true, whatever is noble, whatever is right ... think about such things" (Philippians 4:8, NIV).

3. Request. I also reflected on the many emotions tied to my unhelpful thoughts and how I wanted to feel instead.

"Do not be anxious about anything, but in every situation, by prayer and petition, with thanksgiving, present your requests to God" (Philippians 4:6).

Daily, I walked and asked the Father for help: *May I feel loved. May I feel joy and hope. May I feel courage.* Eventually, I found that *May I ...* was replaced with *I'm grateful that I have joy and hope.* I didn't completely feel it yet, but I could say it, and I trusted God for it. He never let me down.

With that season behind me, I now understand that God led me to *"lie down in green pastures"* (Psalm 23:2, NIV) because I wasn't doing life on my own anymore. He knew I needed Him and the refreshment He brings to my soul. He was asking me to draw closer to Him, to trust Him first, and to focus on the thoughts of the Holy Spirit who dwells inside of me.

Father, You are my Shepherd and my strength. Help me always to recognize Your voice above all others and to turn to You. Let Your thoughts be my thoughts, filling my heart and mind with Your Spirit of Truth so that I might rest in You. In Jesus' Name, Amen.

You Don't Have To Stay Stuck

ERIN WYATT

"I waited patiently for the LORD; And He inclined to me, And heard my cry. He also brought me up out of a horrible pit, Out of the miry clay, And set my feet upon a rock, And *established my steps." Psalm 40:1-2 (NKJV)*

It was the perfect summer morning. The sun was shining, the birds were singing, and my husband, Brian, felt like a kid again as he loaded his newly purchased dirt bike into the bed of the truck. When he was younger, he'd raced dirt bikes but had a terrible accident that halted that hobby for many years. Today was a little bit of redemption. Nothing too crazy, just a nice ride out in the hills with a friend. Or so we thought.

I was thoroughly enjoying my day on our shady backyard patio when I got a call from the wife of this friend, saying, "So I got a message that the guys had an incident. They are OK, but Brian got stuck. Really, really stuck." He needed a change of clothes and towels.

What in the world? I nervously loaded up and headed their way, unsure of what I was going to find when I got there.

I pulled up to see both the dirt bike and my husband covered in mud. Like, up to his chest. Apparently, as his friend rode several yards ahead of where Brian was riding, he didn't see Brian ride straight into a huge sinkhole.

It was disguised by the same dry, cracked dirt as the landscape nearby, but the wet mud underneath him yanked his tires to a stop, and he started sinking. The more he tried to get out, the more the mud pulled him in. Thankfully, his friend finally realized he was missing, went back to see what happened, and painstakingly pulled Brian out of the muck with a rope.

Have you ever felt that stuck? The realization itself can bring with it defeated emotions like panic, loneliness and hopelessness. I've been there. The enemy wants us to believe that there is nothing we can do but surrender to the pit, that no one is coming to help. But we have a friend who finds us there and has the power to pull us out onto solid ground.

Maybe today you find yourself really stuck. Maybe you're stuck in an addiction, a cycle of negative thinking, or depression. Maybe you're just stuck in the overwhelm of daily responsibilities and feel the pressure closing in on you, pulling you under, slowly but surely.

Can I tell you some good news? You absolutely don't have to stay there! Psalm 40:1-2 says, "*I waited patiently for the LORD; And He inclined to me, And heard my cry. He also brought me up out of a horrible pit, Out of the miry clay, And set my feet upon a rock,* And *established my steps.*"

There is someone there to help. He hears when you cry out to Him. He will pull you out of your pit and show you the next steps to take.

Father, I feel stuck, alone and helpless in this pit. I am crying out for Your help. You are my Rescuer — please bring me out of this horrible pit and set my feet on solid ground. Open my eyes and ears to Your direction, and help me clearly understand each next step. Shut the mouth of the enemy who tells me otherwise. I'll wait patiently for You in peace and fully trust You to come through. In Jesus' Name, Amen.

God Rejoices Over You

CARRIE ZEILSTRA

"The LORD your God is in your midst, a mighty one who will save; he will rejoice over you with gladness; he will quiet you by his love; he will exult over you with loud singing." Zephaniah 3:17 (ESV)

A deep sigh escaped my lungs, sounding loud in my dark living room. Another sleepless night was spent reviewing my shortcomings of the day. *Why can't you get it together?* I chided myself. *You're such a mess. You didn't even make your family a decent dinner. The house is cluttered. What is wrong with you?*

My shoulders slumped. Tears rolled down my face. I should have been exhausted, but my inner critic kept me awake … again.

I cried out, *Father, I know You made me. But I am always so behind and scattered. I feel like a failure.*

In the silence, God reminded me of a verse that a friend had shared with me years earlier. But I couldn't remember all the words. Hopeful, I turned on a lamp, found my Bible and searched feverishly. When I found the verse, I whispered it aloud:

"The LORD your God is in your midst, a mighty one who will save; he will rejoice over you with gladness; he will quiet you by his love; he will exult over you with loud singing" (Zephaniah 3:17).

A memory flashed across my mind. I was driving with my toddler in the back seat. In the rearview mirror, I could see my son's head bopping side to side as I sang to him. I sang familiar melodies but replaced the lyrics with his name and fun facts about him. Another glance in the rearview mirror confirmed my son's face was lit up with a big smile, despite the tears on his eyelashes from a tantrum he'd had moments earlier. My heart swelled with love.

The picture in my mind shifted. It was the same scene but with God in the driver's seat, loudly singing a beautiful melody over me.

I read the verse again and whispered a prayer of gratitude. *Thank You that You are with me. You sing over me because I am Your child. You rejoice over me with gladness.* That night, God's song drowned out the negative narrative I spoke to myself. He continues to melt my long-held beliefs about my worth.

I am more than my failures or successes. My worth does not lie in check marks on my to-do list or even in how I perceive myself. My weaknesses don't define me — the God of the universe does! The mighty One says I am worth saving.

Sometimes my mind is still unkind to my heart. But when I choose to focus on the Lord's presence, I picture Him singing over me. Singing my name because He knows me. His song of love quiets my mind.

My heavenly Father reminds me that even when I am wrestling with my thoughts, I am worth saving. Even when I am tempted to think I am lacking, I am His child. Even when I can't see past my shortcomings, He is rejoicing over me in song.

My ears may never hear the notes on this side of eternity, but oh, what a beautiful melody it is.

Dear Lord, quiet my mind with Your love. Let Your song over me be louder than the negative thoughts I may have about who I am. Help me to find my worth in being Your child, not in my untrustworthy feelings. Root me in the knowledge of how wide and long and high and deep Your love is (Ephesians 3:17-19). In Jesus' Name, Amen.

The Searching That Leads to Love

JO CROSBY

"Search me, O God, and know my heart! Try me and know my thoughts! And see if there be any grievous way in me, and lead me in the way everlasting!" Psalm 139:23-24 (ESV)

Years ago, I lost my wedding band. The realization that it was missing came after a full day of activities that included driving home a friend of my daughter's. Noticing the ring's absence, I was upset. Considering it lost, I was heartbroken.

A housewide search ensued. We looked in trash cans and under cushions. We swept floors and stooped down to eye-level with the carpet, hoping to see precious metal reflecting light. Eventually, I stood by the clothes hamper, searching in the pockets of clothes no one had even worn that day. *This is the upside-down, passionate thinking of searching: A thorough search leaves nothing to be missed.*

After the house search turned up empty, I drove to my daughter's friend's home. Flashlight in hand, I searched for the band along the darkened driveway. At midnight, the family's empathy was still holding fast when I sobbed that I would be back in the morning to search in the daylight. *This is the steadfast way of searching: Giving up is not an option. At the heart of searching, there is a passion to find.*

The frenetic searching led to a God-and-me talk on the drive home. I whined. I fretted. Mostly I cried. Thankfully, God is the best at knowing my heart. He sees. He listens. He welcomes tears. He understands. God searches me.

This is the invested, personal nature of God's love: He searches the heart. In relationship with Him, we invite this searching. We welcome being turned upside down and inside out by God. We are glad when God persists, brings His flashlight, or gets eye-level with all that is really going on with our lives. When it comes to our dirty laundry, we give Him the hamper. Being searched and seen by God equates to being known by Him. It is an extension of His care, and His searching affirms our value.

It is easy to think that God doesn't search for us. We can wrongly believe that God's either too busy to look or we are not worth the search. We sometimes reason, *God might love me, but He doesn't really know me.*

These ways of thinking lead to feeling disconnected, ignored or marginalized in relationship with Him. In Psalm 139:23-24, we read one psalmist's request to God: "*Search me, O God, and know my heart! Try me and know my thoughts! And see if there be any grievous way in me, and lead me in the way everlasting!*" The psalmist invited divine searching and embraced the closeness it created between him and God.

When God searches, He finds. God always knows where to look, and He deals directly with the issues at hand. We can invite Him to search us, confidently knowing that His love is steadfast.

I eventually found my wedding ring lying in the bottom of our cat's food bowl. It must have slipped off when I fed her. I was instantly thankful, but the cat seemed unperturbed. She looked at me as if I had fretted over nothing — because she and God had known where it was the whole time.

Father, search my heart with Your steadfast love and care. Remind me that You not only see me but also understand me; help me recognize and refute the thoughts that state otherwise. Lead me to a deeper understanding of both knowing You and being known by You. Thank You for caring so beautifully and personally for me. In Jesus' Name, Amen.

Lather, Rinse, Repeat

BRENDA MORRELL

"… and we take captive every thought to make it obedient to Christ."
2 Corinthians 10:5 (NIV)

I'm a speech writer. In fact, I'm a great speech writer, and my best work is done in the shower. I spew condemning words and relish the imaginary confrontation with someone who has done me wrong. I lather, rinse and repeat for as long as necessary, taking a break only to shake my fist at an invisible face.

I leave nothing out, and nothing is off-limits. By the time I reach for my towel, my soliloquy is perfected, and my mood is perfectly awful.

Thankfully, I have never given one of the speeches that originated in my shower. For that reason, I tried to convince myself long ago that letting my thoughts rage out of control in this way was acceptable. It felt so good to be mad, and I regarded my anger as justified. Besides, I figured no one was getting hurt by my private thoughts.

But the truth is that the raging in my head was not exactly taking captive every thought and making it obedient to Christ (2 Corinthians 10:5).

My little tirades in the shower, without fail, were not so private and innocent. They carried over into my day and into my relationships with the people I love. Everyone around me was affected by my negative attitude as I pointed out faults and snapped at anyone who dared to cross me.

Imaginarily telling someone off is a form of ruminating. Unfortunately, it is the exact opposite of the ruminating God wants us to do. Philippians 4:8 states, "*Finally, brothers and sisters, whatever is true, whatever is noble, whatever is right, whatever is pure, whatever is lovely, whatever is admirable—if anything is excellent or praiseworthy—think about such things*" (NIV).

Dwelling on previous injustices and brooding over past offenses fills up all the spaces in my mind, leaving no room for any of the things listed in that verse. My thought patterns were giving rise to anger and bitterness instead of a humble and forgiving spirit.

And my silent anger wasn't just hurting me. Proverbs 4:23 says, *"Above all else, guard your heart, for everything you do flows from it"* (NIV). When ugliness takes root in my heart, I can be assured that same ugliness will be unleashed in my words and actions. Thinking I can follow Jesus Christ and be obedient to Him while my heart is a breeding ground for resentment is inconsistent indeed.

I am responsible for my thoughts, and each one of them matters. That is why God instructs me to take each one captive. In obedience to Christ, I do have the ability to control my thoughts — and the shower is the perfect place to focus on clean ones.

Now when I am in the shower, I lather, rinse and repeat 2 Corinthians 10:5: "*... and we take captive every thought to make it obedient to Christ.*" (And I make sure my shampoo is the only thing foaming.)

Dear heavenly Father, today I recognize that every thought matters. Release me from the power of Satan's lie that my angry thoughts aren't hurting anyone. Produce in me a humble spirit and a willingness to take every thought captive. I want all of my thinking to reflect Yours so that only pure and lovely things are displayed in my words and actions. In Jesus' Name, Amen.

When Everything Changes, This Remains the Same
LAURA LACEY JOHNSON

"They were looking intently up into the sky as he was going, when suddenly two men dressed in white stood beside them. 'Men of Galilee,' they said, 'why do you stand here looking into the sky? This same Jesus, who has been taken from you into heaven, will come back in the same way you have seen him go into heaven.'" Acts 1:10-11 (NIV)

I sat motionless in the rocking chair.

After eight years of marriage, I couldn't wait to hold the newborn son wriggling in my arms. Yet nothing prepared me for the dizzying change that accompanied motherhood. After an unexpected cesarean section, everything familiar felt like it got thrown into a blender: My body. Work. Sleep. Priorities. Laundry. Schedule. Groceries.

My mother became my security blanket. She was at my side for two weeks, answering my every question, "Am I doing this right?" But when the day came for her to pack up and head home, one paralyzing thought played on repeat: *I have no idea what I'm doing.*

Change is hard. Whether we're moving to a new address, switching jobs, or hearing the words, "It's not you — it's me," adjusting to a new normal can feel scary, unsettling or downright overwhelming.

I imagine that's how the disciples felt in Acts 1:11, where we find them at a complete standstill after Jesus ascended back to heaven. They weren't moving a muscle, and two angels arrived to get them moving:

"... Why do you stand here looking into the sky? This same Jesus, who has been taken from you into heaven, will come back in the same way you have seen him go into heaven" (Acts 1:11).

You and I live between the ascension of Jesus and His glorious return. That tension can be hard. Some days, I want Jesus to rush back and vacuum me out of the pain of this life. Other days, I find myself staring into the clouds like the disciples, confused and a little lost.

Yet it's in this place we must remember: Jesus can make the hardest step forward the best step forward.

When I peeked out the window and saw my mom's taillights, questions pelted my mind:

How can I possibly be a mother?
What if I don't have what it takes?
Can I even keep this tiny human alive?

That's when I heard an unexpected explosion. Stinky, warm poo found its way up my baby's back, down his legs and around my waist.

I had no time to question my calling as a mother. No time to ponder the future. No time to worry that I didn't have what it takes. My next step was finding a bath and a bigger diaper — fast.

Maybe you're cuddling a newborn and wondering if you've even got what it takes to be a parent. Or you're facing a financial crisis that leaves you anxious and afraid you'll never find a way forward. Or you've entered a new stage of life, and you don't know what to do next.

Often the first steps are the hardest. Jesus knew this; that's why He assured His disciples that through the Holy Spirit, He would be with them every step of the way. And He would meet them in the most unexpected and even mysterious ways.

Today, Jesus is with you even though you can't see Him. When everything changes, He stays the same — faithful and true. That always remains the same.

Lord, sometimes I feel overwhelmed by all the changes that have come my way. As I enter each new stage of life, assure me that You will meet me in wonderful and unexpected ways. When I'm uncertain about what to do next, please help me find my way forward. When I question my calling, infuse me with courage and remind me that You will never leave me. I thank You that You are always faithful and true. In Jesus' Name, Amen.

Leaving the Land of Deep Darkness

JUDY THRESHER

"'Lord, help!' they cried in their trouble, and he saved them from their distress. He led them from the darkness and deepest gloom; he snapped their chains." Psalm 107:13-14 (NLT)

As a small child, my blissful feelings of safety were shattered when our peaceful home was broken into and burglarized while we were away.

That would have been enough to send me over the edge — but there was more. The burglar chose my bedroom window to smash into pieces and crawl through.

For several years later, I feared what lurked in the darkness. At the very least, I would sleep with a light on. If I heard noises outside, I would sleep on the floor in my sister's room. Sometimes, it was enough to have the light on, but other times, I needed to know someone else was in the room with me.

Eventually, my fear of darkness dissipated, but dark moments caused by fear of the unknown did not. Anxiety about what was yet to come overwhelmed me.

Oftentimes, overwhelming fear fueled by challenging circumstances, past failures or still-tender wounds can convince us that we are on our own and must face everything alone. We might feel a sense of impending doom, not just for the faraway future but for what could happen in the next hour.

This fear can take the form of constant worries about our relationships, children, work or finances. Worse yet, we can deceive ourselves into believing that our failures may be too much for God. We may even feel that we have exhausted the limits of God's mercy toward us and that since we don't measure up, we will be left to languish in the dark by ourselves.

But that is simply not true. The unfailing Word of God tells us in Psalm 23:6 that His mercy will pursue us all the days of our lives.

Further, we can dwell securely in God's promise that there are no limits or time frames on His guidance and protection of us: "*The LORD will keep you from all harm—he will watch over your life; the LORD will watch over your coming and going both now and forevermore*" (Psalm 121:7-8, NIV).

During our times of despair, the Lord wants us to cry out to Him because He can help lead us out of the dark trap of overwhelming fear and anxiety.

"'*LORD, help!' they cried in their trouble, and he saved them from their distress. He led them from the darkness and deepest gloom; he snapped their chains*" (Psalm 107:13-14).

Friend, God will never forsake us, and especially not at our most vulnerable times. He will stay in the room with us. He will flood our hearts with light, leading us from darkness to a safe place.

Dear Lord, sometimes anxious thoughts weigh me down and leave my heart feeling ravaged. Please fill me with calm in these moments, reminding me that You are here. Thank You that Your mercy follows me not just some days but all the days of my life. I cling to Your promise that You gave in Luke 1:78: "Because of God's tender mercy, the morning light from heaven is about to break upon us ..." *(NLT). In Jesus' Name, Amen.*

Look Up, Child

JESSICA CHAMBERS

"Consider the birds of the sky: They don't sow or reap or gather into barns, yet your heavenly Father feeds them. Aren't you worth more than they?"
Matthew 6:26 (CSB)

Please, God. I can't.

I stood in my kitchen staring blankly out the window. It was another season of depression — a battle I'm familiar with but never prepared for.

It comes with no sleep, no energy, and a barrage of anxiety and fear racing through my mind. Thoughts influence feelings, which become tiny weights that fill my body until it hurts to breathe, each one leading my mind to its inevitable conclusion: *I'm nothing.*

That's where I was that day.

The scene through my window began to come into focus. In my backyard, there were birds everywhere — pecking in the grass, perched in the trees, hopping on the fence. In that moment, Matthew 6:26 was pressed into my heart, drowning the noise in my head:

*"Consider the birds of the sky: They don't sow or reap or gather into barns, yet your heavenly Father feeds them. **Aren't you worth more than they?**"*
(emphasis added).

My mind slowed, and I started to hear the birds singing as I let Jesus' own words sink in.

In Matthew 6:26, Jesus asks us to think about how God cares for His creation. The birds don't plant, harvest or store food for themselves, but God feeds them. They are completely dependent on Him for their every need, and He faithfully provides. It's a promise. And just like every other promise He makes throughout Scripture, He never fails to keep His Word.

In the midst of a battle, a promise can feel far off and empty. But each time God fulfills His promises, He proves His character — that of a sovereign, faithful, unchanging, loving Father and Creator. When we remember who God is and how we can trust Him completely, true peace comes.

That's when I realized I needed to shift from focusing on what I could see in this world to focusing on Him. I needed to look up.

On that day when birds filled my yard, God used this familiar passage to speak to my battle-worn soul — reminding me not just of what He had promised but why I could trust in that promise because of who He is. And I felt my heart settle.

Nothing in my world changed. There was still little sleep or energy. I still felt the weight in my body. But now, there was a comfort. Something that made me feel safe. Three truths I could hold with a white-knuckled grip in the dark: *God is still on the throne. He is still in control. I am still His child.*

That's what I needed to remember. Maybe you need reminding today too.

And in those moments when you forget, He gently lifts your chin and whispers, *I'm still here. Look up, child.*

Father in heaven, thank You that in Your great love and mercy, You meet me where I am to remind me of the hope I have in You. Lord, please help me in this battle to remember that You are with me. Speak truth to my heart so I can have Your peace no matter what is going on in my life. Help me, despite the temptation toward unbelief, to trust You. In Jesus' Name, Amen.

How To Reframe Your Situation

KRISTIN FINCH

"You intended to harm me, but God intended it for good to accomplish what is now being done, the saving of many lives." Genesis 50:20 (NIV)

All of a sudden: bang! A large, white truck in the center lane smashes into the left side of my car. A moment ago, I was singing out of tune to the blasting radio, and now I'm pulling over to check the damage.

Stunned from the crash, my mind begins to race. I feel myself start to panic. *How could this happen? What do I do next? Why didn't that driver see me?*

I reach for my phone and then pause. This crash could have gone a whole lot worse. Breathing in slowly as the tears flow, I whisper, *Thank You, Jesus, for protecting me.*

No one can ever anticipate the unexpected, inconvenient car crashes of life. They happen to everyone — and Joseph in the Bible was no exception.

Joseph would eventually lead a nation, but what he didn't know ahead of time was that he would endure many challenging situations along the way. He never expected that he would be sold into slavery by his own brothers and later sent to prison (Genesis 37; Genesis 39).

I love the part in Joseph's story when he was reunited with his brothers and became a great leader after many years of hardship. He said to his brothers, "*You intended to harm me, **but God** intended it for good to accomplish what is now being done, the saving of many lives*" (Genesis 50:20, emphasis added).

Joseph could have stayed stuck in bitterness and repaid his brothers for the evil they did. Instead, he said "*but God*" and chose to believe that what happened to him was for good — even though it didn't seem good in the moment. God was working everything out to fulfill His purpose in Joseph's life even when Joseph couldn't see it.

What if we choose to believe that our painful experiences are actually leading us to our destiny? What if we reframed our situation by adding "but God"?

"This isn't what I thought it would be, but God sustains me."
"I don't have what it takes, but God is my strength."
"I feel brokenhearted, but God is my comforter."

We can take a lesson from Joseph and be encouraged that no matter what happens, God is a promise keeper. When you add "but God" and focus on His character instead of the situation in front of you, God will replace thoughts of anger, fear or worry with thoughts of joy, peace and goodness.

Your circumstances may not change immediately or even on this side of eternity. But you can focus on what Scripture says: God will always work all things for the good of those who love Him, who have been called according to His purpose (Romans 8:28). This will help reframe any self-defeating, negative thoughts because you can trust God has a great purpose and plan perfectly designed for you.

Dear Jesus, thank You for always loving me unconditionally. This situation in front of me is challenging, yet although it may not seem good, I can say: "But God is greater than anything I am facing." I trust You and believe the plans You have for me will be for good. Help me focus on who You are and the great purpose You have ahead for my life. Help me to see Your faithfulness and goodness through it all. In Jesus' Name, Amen.

Replace Limiting Thoughts With God's Thoughts

YVONNE PEREZ

"He said to them, 'Cast the net on the right side of the boat, and you will find some.' So they cast it, and now they were not able to haul it in, because of the quantity of fish." John 21:6 (ESV)

When my children were younger and found themselves overwhelmed by a task that seemed bigger than their ability, my husband would always ask them, "How do you eat an elephant?"

It seemed like a ridiculous question to them at first, for obvious reasons. But the answer was simple and always gave them the confidence they needed. He'd tell them, "One bite at a time." And with that, they would take on whatever challenge was ahead of them, one step at a time.

I still ask myself that same question when problems seem bigger than my abilities to solve them and the enemy magnifies every feeling of my perceived inadequacies. Often, quitting feels easier than pressing on after I've poured everything into something that just seems to fall apart. Sometimes I give in to circumstances that seem impossible, and other times, I forsake trying before even beginning. I succumb to the doubts in my head that taunt me, telling me that I'm not capable or qualified.

Maybe that's how the Apostle Peter felt as he was washing his nets the morning after fishing all night and catching nothing. He might have been discouraged as he was giving up and packing up. Sometimes our best efforts don't yield the outcome we desire, and it's easy to surrender to defeat like Peter.

But if we look back on John 21, Jesus didn't allow Peter to give up. He didn't console Peter and tell him to try another day. In fact, it was the opposite. In John 21:6a, after Peter had confirmed he hadn't caught any fish, Jesus said, *"Cast the net on the right side of the boat, and you will find some."* When Peter obeyed, he caught so many fish he could barely pull them in. Because Peter didn't doubt, Jesus enabled him to accomplish something amazing.

It's easy to look at our flawed circumstances and give in to the lies in our minds that keep us from trusting what God has already made possible. But in 2 Corinthians 10:5, God urges us to take our thoughts captive continually: "*We demolish arguments and every pretension that sets itself up against the knowledge of God, and we take captive every thought to make it obedient to Christ*" (NIV).

This simply means replacing our limiting thoughts with God's thoughts. When we do, we become transformed into the people God created us to be. We are capable of more than our thoughts suggest and are able to hear God in the moments He tells us to try something a different way.

When our thoughts are in alignment with God's, the enemy has no hold on us. The enemy's plan to discourage us and lead us away from God's calling on our lives is rendered useless. By taking captive our limiting thoughts and replacing them with God's Truth, we find the key to overcoming negative thoughts.

Lord, I thank You that I'm not alone in the battle of my thoughts. Thank You that Your guidance is always there when I need it. I know that my thoughts can sometimes try to convince me that I'm unqualified or unworthy of what You have placed before me. Please help me to take my thoughts captive continually and make them obedient to Christ so that I can walk in Your will and glorify You. In Jesus' Name, Amen.

Finding Peace Amid Mental Dysregulation
TERRI PORTER

"You keep him in perfect peace whose mind is stayed on you, because he trusts in you." Isaiah 26:3 (ESV)

Quietness creeps into the house. It's midnight and I'm awake. I've scoured the homestead for every piece of laundry that even looks like it needs to be washed. Busyness is my distraction of the moment.

Is the phone going to ring? Will it be the cops?

In between loads, dishes are noiselessly added to the dishwasher, a roast is prepped for the crockpot, and the coffee maker is programmed to enable me to drag myself out of bed in just a few hours. Lists checked off temporarily soothe my brain.

Why doesn't she answer my texts? Is she safe?

I glance at the clock — it's 1 a.m., and my thoughts are betraying me. I pace around the dinner table. I hate the nighttime. It's always at night.

My prodigal child has not yet come home. My heart constricts.

Have you ever found yourself in a similar moment, attempting to humanly create peace? Or maybe struggling to maintain stability despite anxiety-filled thought disruptions?

Well, as a flesh-and-blood human being, I have found myself on the struggle bus of having worrisome thoughts cascade through my brain.

Thankfully, we have a map in Scripture navigating us along the pathway where mental peace can be acquired. It's found in Isaiah 26:3: *"You keep him in perfect peace whose mind is stayed on you, because he trusts in you."* The truths found in this verse can help establish habits necessary for maintaining a sound thought life even in the thick of trauma.

One of the first things we notice amid a crisis is the evaporation of peace. Yet God makes this promise to *"keep [us] in perfect peace."*

Notice it's not just peace but *"perfect peace."* In Hebrew, the word "shalom" is repeated twice here. Its basic meaning is completeness or wholeness. It was traditionally used as a greeting and a blessing, spoken like a prayer for a person's complete well-being. It does not simply mean inner peace of mind but also peace with God and peace with all humankind. Shalom carries the idea of complete health, including soundness of mind.

You see, God's peace is a total package of wellness that preserves our mental health. I like that God started this verse with the promise of peace and then led into the "how." He gave the guarantee first and then unveiled the instructions: *"... whose mind is stayed on you, because he trusts in you"* (Isaiah 26:3).

In order to secure this promised peace, we have to wrangle the thought patterns of our minds. It's not easy and takes practice, but the promise of perfect peace is a grand motivator.

꙰ First, ground your thoughts by studying the character of God. This will establish a core of trust in His abilities, His will, and His faithfulness to you as a child of God (Psalm 116:5).

꙰ Next, meditate on the characteristics of God. Ruminate over them. Post them in places you frequent (Psalm 84:11-12).

꙰ Then speak those truths out loud, bringing your thoughts into line with the truths of God's Word (Isaiah 55:11).

With these things in mind, I was able to go to sleep before my prodigal child returned home that night. God kept her safe and well.

Lord, I am choosing to trust Your faithfulness today. Thank You for offering me Your peace when mine is gone. Despite my circumstances, I am fixing my mind on the truths of Your promises. I choose to rest in Your perfect peace. In Jesus' Name, Amen.

When Shame Takes You for a Spin

MANDY JOHNSON

"See what kind of love the Father has given to us, that we should be called children of God; and so we are. The reason why the world does not know us is that it did not know him." 1 John 3:1 (ESV)

"Let's sit down for lunch!" my friend said.

With an overflowing stroller and energetic toddler, I fumbled my way over to a wooden picnic table in the park. My two mom friends reached into their diaper bags and pulled out pink and purple plastic plates with lids, along with matching utensils and water cups, then laid everything out on our table like we were about to partake in a holiday feast.

They peeled off the lids of their lunch plates with care, revealing perfectly cut sandwiches with nothing oozing out of the sides, dollops of fresh hummus, bright red strawberries, and ripe green cucumber slices cut in the shape of Mickey Mouse. Not only did my friends arrive more than prepared for their children, but they also made beautiful lunches for themselves.

I don't want to pull our food out of my diaper bag, I thought, but my son wanted to eat, especially after seeing the pristine lunches his friends had. I reached into my bag and pulled out a black hand-me-down lunchbox filled with a random assortment of things I had grabbed on my way out of the house. String cheese, a protein bar, pretzels, and a crumbled white napkin stared me in the face as shame jumped on the opportunity to take my thoughts for a spin.

I'm not a good mom.
I don't measure up to these moms.
I'm a disappointment to my son.

Whether you're a mother or not, the temptation to feel shame for not meeting spoken or unspoken social expectations is real, and it's challenging to recover from. Maybe you're the single girl who learns yet another friend is engaged, the corporate go-getter who is passed over for a promotion, or the mom who lets worldly pressures steal her joy … One lie at a time, shame can erode our confidence in our decisions and our identity.

Shame leaves us thinking we aren't valuable, capable or faithful enough in our unique roles. But God tells us that in Him, the opposite is true.

First John 3:1 says, *"See what kind of love the Father has given to us, that we should be called children of God; and so we are. The reason why the world does not know us is that it did not know him."*

Friend, if you trust in Christ, you are a child of God. Let that sink in. You can squash every shame-filled thought creeping into your mind with the love of one name: Jesus.

The next time you're in one of those all-too-familiar low moments, questioning your worth and feeling tempted to think you don't measure up as an individual, friend, wife, daughter or mother, I encourage you to pause and remember the truth about who you really are: chosen, called, cherished. Shame fights to show you that you're never enough. Jesus died to show you that He's always enough. Through Him, you have everything you need.

Father God, thank You for calling me Your daughter. Help me remember and believe how valuable I am in Your eyes. Give me an awareness of my thoughts when I'm tempted to let shame take over. Fill me with confidence in You. In Jesus' Name, Amen.

When Change Becomes a Challenge

JOY A. WILLIAMS

"'For the mountains may depart and the hills be removed, but my steadfast love shall not depart from you, and my covenant of peace shall not be removed,' says the LORD, who has compassion on you." Isaiah 54:10 (ESV)

When I learned a close friend was moving overseas, my heart sank. Instead of meeting in our church's lobby after the service, we would have to meet over the internet. The distance brought uncertainty because when change comes, a challenge is often not far behind.

Not knowing what comes next can stifle my ability to walk by faith. As my sense of vulnerability heightens, my mind shifts toward worst-case scenarios. And my soul becomes desperate for God.

In the midst of change, I'm comforted by God's promise in Isaiah 54:10. It was written to desperate people who had lost their freedom. They had lost loved ones, and often they lost their devotion to God.

However, as Israel returned from being exiled in Babylonian captivity, this was God's response: *"'For the mountains may depart and the hills be removed, but my steadfast love shall not depart from you, and my covenant of peace shall not be removed,' says the LORD, who has compassion on you"* (Isaiah 54:10).

Mountains and hills moving certainly would have changed the Israelites' view. It can change our perspective too. Mountains and hills represent varying heights of stability, but they are a part of creation. By earthquake or explosion, they can be shaken. They can be moved.

Similarly, the stability of a relationship, a career or our resources can start to crumble before our eyes. The hills of a promising scenario can go from being hopeful to becoming a hurt that won't let go. But as we make our Creator our priority, His stability comes to us (Psalm 16:8).

He gave Israel new hope for a new season. He had compassion on them and led them from captivity. He also has compassion on us. He desires to help us take captive our worst-case-scenario thoughts (2 Corinthians 10:4-5) and leads us to His hope-filled promises.

Even when life changes, God never will. His love for us doesn't change (Romans 8:38-39). His Word doesn't change (Numbers 23:19). His Son doesn't change: *"Jesus Christ is the same yesterday and today and forever"* (Hebrews 13:8, ESV).

To all who believe in Him, Christ offers us God's new covenant of peace (Hebrews 9:14-15). When change is our biggest challenge, it's still no match for His redemption.

Inevitably, change comes to us all. Sadly, sometimes we're unable to alter what causes a difficulty. But through Christ, we can experience wisdom, comfort and strength even in circumstances we hoped to avoid. His steadfast love shall not depart from us. His covenant of peace shall not be removed. Each time a transition happens, it leads us to our next season of trusting God.

For me, it's been a few years since my friend's relocation. Now, several emails and a few visits later, there's no longer any fear of the distance. Our families continue to marvel at the faithfulness of God.

Lord, the seasons of life often change. Thank You for Your steadfast love and the covenant of peace we have in Jesus. No matter how we see life's transitions, help us to see You. May we choose to take captive our worst-case-scenario thoughts and cling to Your hope-filled promises. In Jesus' Name, Amen.

You Just Need a Tiny Speck of Faith

GLENDA FERNANDO

"And he said to her, 'Daughter, your faith has made you well; go in peace, and be healed of your disease.'" Mark 5:34 (ESV)

Another night of lying in bed and not finding sleep. My mind is racing with worries about my children and their future, my husband and his job, my sister and her recent battle with cancer. My mind is condemning me for not being a better mother, wife, daughter, friend. My mind is recounting conversations, which bring on shame because I said too much, too little, the wrong words. My mind is deceiving me into thinking I am not good enough and am unworthy of love.

This nightly ritual of my mind spiraling has been haunting me for years, too many to count. On good nights, I find relief in sleep. On bad nights, I remain in this endless spiral with no hope of sleep.

One hopeless night, I recalled a woman in Scripture who I am sure had many hopeless nights of her own — 12 years of them, in fact, as she suffered from an illness that was socially stigmatized in her culture (Mark 5:25-26). Yet in a moment, the touch of Jesus calmed her mind, her thoughts and her soul and healed her body.

She just wanted a little piece of Jesus. She was so desperate that she knew if she just had a little part, maybe, just maybe, He would give her relief. Her desperation propelled her forward to Jesus, who she believed would help her in her time of need. She pushed aside her years of shame and humiliation to seek Him. But she didn't make a huge declaration. She just quietly reached out and touched the hem of His garment (Mark 5:27-29).

Because of that tiny bit of faith, Jesus told her, *"Daughter, your faith has made you well; go in peace"* (Mark 5:34).

Those words must have sent shock waves through her body and mind, healing her and calming her soul. Can you imagine? Just a moment before, she was in the midst of her hopeless, shameful situation. Then instantly, her world changed. Because of her tiny speck of faith, her life was completely different. Her spiral ended.

Could Jesus end my spiral, too, with just a bit of faith? At times, my thoughts make my mind so clouded that I don't think I have any options. I feel that my negative thoughts are overpowering my life and there is no hope, no relief. I feel my faith dissipating, which causes my spiral to deepen. However, Jesus shows that just a speck of faith can heal you and me.

So in the midst of our negative thoughts, let's take a fragment of faith and reach out for Jesus. In the midst of our shame, we, too, can be healed.

The same power that healed the woman in Mark 5 is available to us. Just reach out and find the hem of Jesus' garment in your mind. Jesus will turn and say, *Daughter, your faith has made you well. Go in peace.*

Jesus, my Savior and Lord, thank You for knowing my heart and my hurt. Help me to remember that my little bit of faith is rewarded with Your great strength and power. Heal me and calm my negative thoughts. Replace them with the truth that I am Your precious and loved daughter. Help me to rest in the peace that only You can provide. In Jesus' Name, Amen.

Sometimes We Need To Do Less and Believe More

VALEEN HAYKIN

"Immediately the father of the child cried out and said, 'I believe; help my unbelief!'" Mark 9:24 (ESV)

I failed my daughters. Again. *Why did I just yell? What happened to the patience I used to have? Will my kids be OK? Will I be OK?*

Jesus, I need You so much right now.

Tears dripped down my cheeks as I rested my chin on top of my sweet daughter's head. I pulled her in tight and whispered, "I'm sorry, baby. Mama loves you so much."

Postpartum depression affects up to 20% of mothers, and sadly, after I welcomed my newest daughter in January 2022, I became part of that statistic. Though I couldn't see the light at the end of the tunnel, God met me in that deep, dark place.

As a busy mama with two kids under 2 years old, I felt my relationship with God begin to become distant. With little time to study my Bible, pray or spend time with Him, my negative thoughts slowly seeped to the surface. *Will I ever be good enough?*

My counselor asked me a series of life-changing questions: "What does 'good enough' even mean? What does it look like? Is it realistic? Did God put those demands on you, or did you?"

As we invite Jesus into our hearts, confessing Him as Savior of our lives, we simply need to believe what we confess. Other than Jesus' sacrifice on the cross, God requires no additional sacrifice to save us. We are His beloved children. Just like the father we meet in Mark 9, sometimes we need to do less and believe more.

The father was in a hopeless state, telling Jesus that a demon had possessed his son for all of his life. Jesus said if the father believed in Him, healing could happen (Mark 9:17-23). "*Immediately the father of the child cried out and said, 'I believe; help my unbelief!*'" (Mark 9:24).

God loves us so much in the undone, imperfect and incomplete places where we find ourselves. Just like the healing of the son in this story, I began my healing journey with a few simple words: *God, I believe. Help my unbelief. I want to believe that I'm worthy of love and that I'm a good mom. I want to believe that I don't need to do anything more to be accepted. I want to believe I can be healed and get better.*

But what happens when it feels like you no longer have time to sit at Jesus' feet? When you can't find your Bible, your notecards with scriptures on them are missing, your journal has been scribbled on, and praying feels like one more chore on the to-do list? Whisper: *Jesus, help me believe.* He will help you rediscover rhythms of devotion to Him.

Jesus sometimes calls us into dark places so we can cling to His light. He wants us to learn that sometimes we need to do less and believe more.

You are God's prized possession, His beloved daughter. You do not have to do one more thing to gain His love and affection. Simply believe.

Dear Jesus, thank You so much for the gift of Your love. God, I stand in agreement with Your Word, and I declare that I believe You. Help me to unpack and uproot all areas of unbelief in my heart that are interfering with me having a real relationship with You. Transform my heart from the inside out, Lord. I believe that I am perfectly loved by You. In Jesus' Name, Amen.

Suffering Can Be the Greatest Gift

LESLIE SEYDLER

"And he said to him, 'You shall love the Lord your God with all your heart and with all your soul and with all your mind. This is the great and first commandment.'" Matthew 22:37-38 (ESV)

I began to feel the unmistakable tightness in my chest and struggled to draw a full breath. All I wanted was to fill my lungs with air and breathe fully. Shaking through the shallow breaths, I laid my head down and wept to God to save and help me.

For seven years, I suffered from a breathing disorder. Doctors were puzzled by it, and traditional remedies brought no relief. Finally, after a long season of waiting and praying, God led me to a specialized clinic where I started to see improvement and get some answers.

During those years, I wrestled with the purpose of the suffering. I felt like Jacob, broken and bruised in the ultimate WWE match with the Lord (Genesis 32:22-32). I questioned, I cried, I threw toddler-level fits, and I doubted God's goodness. I believed the lie that suffering meant God had abandoned me.

Jesus lovingly met me in that pit and began to reveal some of the purpose in my suffering. I thought I needed a medical breakthrough, but God knew what I needed most was Him. Because of suffering, I learned to seek the Lord. I had been a Christian for many years, but never had I hungered for God like this.

Breathing room came long before the physical healing. Breathing room came when I learned to love Him more than anything else. Loving Him most brings freedom from despair even in seemingly hopeless situations.

When asked what the greatest commandment is, Jesus said, *"You shall love the Lord your God with all your heart and with all your soul and with all your mind. This is the great and first commandment"* (Matthew 22:37-38).

This is the greatest commandment because it is the fulfillment of God's law and is the ultimate prize and aim of life. Loving God gives us the power to overcome because God becomes our life, our longing, our every breath. Fear has no power over us when our greatest aim is to know God more than to be rescued.

Friend, this is a process that God meets us in. No effort in pursuing the heart of God is ever wasted. Daily we pray and study the Scripture and ask God to help us know and love Him more. Daily He is faithful to restore us and show us who He is. Slowly, we are transformed and begin to understand that everything in life of value and of worth is from Him and for Him. Suffering can be the greatest gift when it leads us to experience intimacy with God like never before.

In longing to breathe, I learned to long for my Savior first. The more we seek after God, the most beautiful exchange of wills happens. Our earthly desires fade into the background, and the joy of being close to God and loving God is the ultimate prize. Nothing else fills us more than God Himself — not even the answers we so ardently seek.

Dear Lord, some days it is so hard to see the purpose of suffering. I long for rescue, but, Lord, teach me to long for You most. I ask that You would reveal Yourself to me and uproot any lies in my mind that are opposed to the truth of Your goodness. Thank You, Lord, for the peace and space that so blessedly comes into my life as I seek after You. I pray that my heart would long for You above all else. In Jesus' Name, Amen.

NOTES

resources

Proverbs 31 Ministries' *Therapy & Theology* podcast

The American Association of Christian Counselors
Visit AACC.net.
This site can help you find a counselor in your area by zip code.

American Foundation for Suicide Prevention
afsp.org

National Suicide Prevention Lifeline
Visit https://988lifeline.org or call 1-800-273-8255.
You can also text "MHA" to 741-741.
This will connect you to a trained counselor from the Crisis Text Line.

The Hotline
Visit thehotline.org or call 1-800-799-7233 (-SAFE).
The site offers anonymous help or practical next steps for those facing
domestic violence or abuse.

*"Grace to you and peace from God our Father and the
Lord Jesus Christ. Blessed be the God and Father of our
Lord Jesus Christ, the Father of mercies and God of
all comfort, who comforts us in all our affliction ..."*

(2 CORINTHIANS 1:2-4. ESV)